ADULT ONLY FISHING JOKES

Guaranteed to make you giggle!

Joke Compilation: Scribblers and Writers
Cover Design: Sam Grimmer
Illustrations: John Shakespeare
Editor: Jasmine Chan
Typesetting: Midland Typesetters, Maryborough, Vic, Australia

HINKLER BOOKS
Adults Only Fishing Jokes
First published in 2004 by Hinkler Books Pty Ltd
17-23 Redwood Drive
Dingley Victoria 3172 Australia
www.hinklerbooks.com.au

First printed in 2004

ISBN 1 7412 1660 5

Printed and bound in Australia

INTRODUCTION

TALL tales, exaggerations and just sheer out-and-out lies—ah, the glorious life of the fisherman.

Fishermen know no bounds. Marriage, relationship, a job, indeed, anything requiring responsibility, will not get in the way of a fisherman and his endeavours to snare that elusive barramundi on a minimal breaking-strain line.

Fishermen live, dream and eat . . . fish.

They can't wait to get up first thing in the morning, wake up the house, the hotel, the entire caravan park or wherever it is they are staying, to head out into the cold and gloom of the early dawn to try their luck.

They spend thousands on equipment, boats and bait—but rarely clothes. A tea cosy will do as a hat.

All in the pursuit of the next biggest catch.

And of course, their endeavours are synonymous with humour—as this book of fishing jokes shows.

We hope you enjoy the catch!

AWAY WE GO!

'Do you really believe your husband when he tells you he goes fishing every weekend?' asked Jane's best friend.

'Why shouldn't I?' said Jane.

'Well, maybe he is having an affair?'

'No way,' said Jane, 'he never returns with any fish . . .'

An Irish fisherman's last wish was to be buried at sea, which was most unfortunate for his three friends who died digging the grave.

The difference between a fairy tale and a fish story is a fairy tale begins, 'Once upon a time' and a fish story begins, 'This ain't no bullshit . . .'

A wealthy fisherman needed a brain transplant.

His doctor told him he only had two brains on hand.

One was of a college professor and cost $10,000.

The other was of a fisherman and cost $500,000.

'You're kidding me Doc! It costs $500,000 for a fisherman's brain. That's awfully expensive.'

'Ah', said the doctor, 'but it's never been used.'

You'll never hear a fisherman's wife say, 'Shouldn't you be down at the bar with your friends?'

A couple of fishermen are out fishing when one of them suddenly grabs his chest and falls to the ground.

He doesn't seem to be breathing and his eyes are rolled back in his head.

The other guy whips out his mobile phone and rings emergency. He gasps to the operator, 'I think Bob is dead! What should I do?'

The operator, in a calm soothing voice says, 'Just take it easy and follow my instructions. First, let's make sure he's dead.'

There is a silence and then a shot is heard.

Then the guy's voice comes back on the line, 'Okay, he's dead.'

I got a new rod and reel for my wife.
Best trade I ever made.

DICTIONARY OF FISHING TERMS

Angler
A stark-racing obsessed individual who resides in a house that is falling down due to neglect, drives a truck whose colour can best be described as crappo-rust-red and who adores a pristine boat that he rubs down with a chamois methodically before and after each trip.

Tackle
What your last catch did to you as you reeled him in, but just before he wrestled free and jumped back overboard.

Lure
An object that is semi-enticing to fish, but will drive an angler into such a frenzy that he will charge his credit card to the limit before exiting the tackle shop.

Sinker
A weight attached to a lure to get it to the bottom; or the nickname for your boat.

Hook
A curved piece of metal used to catch fish; or a clever advertisement to entice a fisherman to spend his life savings on a new rod and reel; or the punch administered by said fisherman's wife after he spends their life savings (see also, Right Hook, Left Hook).

Thumb
A temporary hook holder.

Treble Hook
Triples the odds of catching a fish. Quadruples the odds of getting the hook caught in your thumb (see above).

Line
Something you give your co-workers when they ask on Monday how your fishing went the past weekend.

Rod
An attractively painted length of fibreglass that keeps an angler from ever getting too close to a fish.

Reel
A weighted object that causes a rod to sink quickly when dropped overboard.

Tackle Box
A box shaped alarmingly like your comprehensive first aid kit. Only a tackle box contains many sharp objects, so that when you reach in the wrong box blindly to get a Band Aid, you soon find that you need more than one.

Trawling
What you do after you've lost a $500 rod and reel set-up overboard.

School
A grouping in which fish are taught to avoid your $29.99 lures and hold out for burley instead.

Test

The amount of strength a fishing line affords an angler when fighting fish in a specific weight range; or a measure of your creativity in blaming that darn line for once again losing the fish.

Catch and Release

A conservation motion that happens most often right before the local Fish and Game officer pulls over a boat that has caught over its limit.

Knot

An insecure connection between your hook and fishing line; or a permanent tangle on your spinning reel which forces you to go out and buy a bigger, better, much more expensive rig.

Landing Net

A net used to help drag a large wiggling fish or an inebriated fishing buddy, on board.

Live Bait

The biggest fish you'll handle all day.

Quiet Water

Your surroundings after you stop cursing your bad luck and fall asleep at the reel.

Skunk

One who returns to the boat ramp many, many hours after his mates have gone home so that there are no witnesses.

YOU GOTTA LAUGH

Q: Why was the sailor buried at sea?
A: Because he was dead.

A young deckhand was being put through the paces by an old sea captain.

'What would you do if a sudden storm sprang up on the starboard?'

'Throw out an anchor, sir,' the student replied.

'What would you do if another storm sprang up aft?'

'Throw out another anchor, sir.'

'And if another terrific storm sprang up forward, what would you do then?' asked the captain.

'Throw out another anchor, sir.'

'Hold on,' said the captain. 'Where are you getting all those anchors from?'

'From the same place you're getting your storms, sir.'

There was an old sailor from Wales,
An expert at pissing in gales.
He could piss in a jar
From the top-gallant spar
Without even wetting the sails.

'Anyone who can guess how many fish I have in this sack can have both of them,' said Murphy.

'Three,' said Tom.

'That's near enough,' said Murphy.

At 3am, the manager of the local fisherman's club receives a phone call at home from a man who sounds quite drunk.

The man asks the manager, 'What time does the club open?'

The manager says, 'Noon,' and he hangs up.

An hour later the phone rings again and the same voice asks, 'What time does the club open?'

Again, the manager says, 'Noon' and hangs up.

At 6.30 the phone rings and the same voice asks, 'Wenja shay the club opens at?'

The manager, now quite peeved, yells, 'I told you before, it opens at noon. And if you don't sober up, you won't be allowed to get in.'

The slurry, drunken voice then says, 'Ah don' wanna get in, I wanna get out.'

Policeman: 'You're not allowed to fish here.'

Boy: 'I'm not fishing. I'm giving my pet worm a bath.'

Policeman: 'You need a permit to catch fish.'

Boy: 'What's wrong with worms?'

A father and son went fishing one summer day.

While they were out in their boat, the boy suddenly became curious about the world around him.

He asked his father, 'Dad, how does this boat float?'

The father replied, 'Don't rightly know, son.'

A little later, the boy looked at his father and asked, 'Dad, how do fish breathe underwater?'

Once again the father replied, 'Don't rightly know, son.'

A little later the boy asked his father, 'Dad, why is the sky blue?'

Again, the father replied, 'Don't rightly know, son.'

Finally, the boy asked his father, 'Dad, do you mind my asking you all of these questions?'

The father replied, 'Of course not, son. If you don't ask questions, you never learn nothing.'

The fire brigade phones the president of the local fishing club, in the early hours of Sunday morning.

'Mr Graham sir, the club rooms are on fire!'

'The cups, man! Save the cups!' cries George.

'Uh, the fire hasn't spread to the canteen yet, sir.'

1st Angler: 'I tell you, it was so long. I never saw another fish like it.'
2nd Angler: 'I believe you.'

A drunken fisherman was seen crawling down some railroad tracks.

Asked if there was a problem, he replied, 'Yeah, can you help me off this ladder.'

George Bush and Al Gore went fishing.

To make it interesting they had a bet about who could catch the most fish.

So, Gore heads out to one side of the lake and Bush goes to the other.

Later that day they return for the count.

Bush came back with 129 fish, Gore caught nothing.

Incensed Gore called for a re-count.

So the next day they head out again.

This time Bush returns with 173 fish and once again, Gore did not catch a thing.

Gore screamed for a re-vote.

He just could not understand it. He was sure that Bush must have been cheating.

So on the third day, Gore decided to send a secret service agent to spy on Bush.

This day Gore once again caught nothing, but Bush came back with 293 fish!

Gore pulls the secret service agent over and asks whether Bush is cheating.

'Yes,' replied the spy, 'he's putting holes in the ice.'

Fishing is the 2nd greatest thrill known to man. Catching a fish is the 1st.

A fisherman died in poverty and many locals donated to a fund for his funeral. The owner of a home at the local lake was asked to contribute a dollar. 'A dollar,' she said, 'only a dollar to bury a fisherman? Here's a cheque, go bury a thousand of them.'

Ben, a local fisherman, went into his favourite bar and ordered six double vodkas.

Bob, the bartender said, 'Wow, Ben, you must have had a bad day.'

'Yeah,' said Ben, 'I just found out my older brother is gay.'

The next day Ben showed up and again ordered six doubles.

Bob said, 'What, more problems?'

And Ben replied, 'Damn right, I just found out that my younger brother is gay.'

The third day, the same routine again—six doubles.

Bob said, 'What the hell, doesn't anyone in your family like women?'

'Yeah,' said Ben, 'I just found out my wife does . . .'

IT'S TRUE!

Give a man a fish and feed him for a day. Teach a man to fish and he will sit in a boat and drink beer all day.

Which fisherman was it that said:
'Outside of a dog, a book is man's best friend.
Inside of a dog, it's too dark to read . . .'

Q: What is the richest fish in the world?
A: A goldfish.

Q: Where does a fish end up when it flies?
A: A magic carp.

Q: What do you call a small fish magician?
A: A magic carpet.

Q: What do fish use for money?
A: Sand dollars.

David, the fisherman, had driven by the lake many times and had seen some other anglers about, so he decided to give his luck a try.

On his first day of fishing he had no luck at all but noticed that another fisherman near him was scooping in one after another.

He had to know 'The Secret'.

'Excuse me sir, but would you mind telling me what sort of bait you are using?' he asked.

The other man looked around a bit embarrassed. 'Well, I am a surgeon and quite by accident I found that the human tonsil works very well.'

David thanked the man, thought about what sort of bait to try next time and left.

The next day, David returned to the lake, tried a different bait and still had no luck. Just as the day before, there was yet a different man reeling in fish after fish.

'Excuse me,' asked David, 'but could you suggest a bait that I could try?'

'Well, I can, but I am not sure it will do you any good. I am using a bit of human appendix.'

'Hmm,' thought David.

It seemed that the fish in this lake would require a little more effort than normal.

He left, willing to give the lake one more try.

On the third day, David still had no luck.

As was usual, there was yet another man near him bringing in fish left and right. David wanted to confirm what he already knew.

'Excuse me sir, but are you a doctor?'

'No, I am a Rabbi,' replied the man.

A man is out in his little fishing row boat when suddenly a passing speed boat raises huge waves and the man's oars fall overboard.

He is stranded out in the middle of the lake!

After about two hours, he sees another row boat going by with a man and two women in it!

The first man yells, 'Hey buddy, can I borrow one of your oars?'

The other man yells back, 'They're not whores . . . one's my wife and one's my sister!'

An elderly fisherman was at home, dying in bed, when he smelled his favourite aroma—chocolate chip biscuits baking.

He wanted one last cookie before he died, so he crawled to the kitchen, reached up to the cookie sheet on the table and grasped a warm, moist chip.

His wife suddenly hit his hand with a spatula and yelled, 'Leave them alone. They're for the funeral.'

Two fishermen were talking about the good old days.

The first one says, 'When I was a kid there were so many fish here I could always catch a few.'

The other says, 'When I was a kid here we used a horse and cart and got enough fish to sell at the market.'

'How did you do that then?'

'Well, we had this good old horse and we used to back the cart down into the water and put treacle on his tail. The flies got stuck in the treacle and when the fish jumped out of the water for the flies that good old horse just kicked them into the cart. We had a load of fish in no time!'

A taxidermist was driving through the country when he thought he would stop at a local bar and have a beer.

The locals didn't like outsiders in their bar and when he entered he was greeted with dirty stares and low mumbles.

He went to the bartender and asked for a beer.

The bartender looked the man over and then went to get his beer.

When the bartender returned with his beer he asked the man, 'What do you do?'

The man replied, 'I'm a taxidermist.'

The bartender replied, 'Taxidermist? What is that?'

The man replied, 'Well, I mount animals, birds and fish.'

With that said the bartender turned to the other men in the bar and said, 'It's okay, boys, he's one of us'.

THEN THERE WAS . . .

A cop pulls a guy over for speeding and the guy's defence was, 'I was just going with the flow of traffic.'

The cop's response . . . 'Ever go fishing?'

'Yeah . . .'

'Ever catch ALL the fish?'

I was glad when one fish got away. There just wasn't room in the boat for both of us!

Q: Which fish can perform operations?
A: A sturgeon!

Q: What is the difference between a fish and a piano?
A: You can't tuna fish.

You know you're staying at a second rate fishing hotel when you call the front desk and say, 'I've got a leak in my sink,' and they say, 'Go ahead.'

A couple of women were fishing one sunny afternoon by a lake.

The first of the two rigged her line with a giant hook and a huge sinker, cast her line and watched in horror as the hook, line and sinker headed directly towards a couple of fishermen nearby.

Sure enough, the sinker hit one of the guys and he immediately clasped his hands together at his crotch, fell to the ground and proceeded to roll around in agony.

The woman rushed over and immediately began to apologise.

She then explained that she was a physical therapist and offered to help ease his pain. 'No thanks, I'll be alright . . . I'll be fine in a few minutes,' he replied as he remained in the foetal position still clasping his hands together at his crotch.

But she persisted and he finally allowed her to help him.

She gently took his hands away and laid them to the side, loosened his pants and put her hands inside, beginning to massage him.

'Does that feel better?' she asked.

'Oh, yeah . . . It feels really great,' he replied, 'But my thumb still hurts like hell!'

Q: What is the difference between a catfish and a lawyer?
A: One is a bottom-dwelling, scum-sucking scavenger and the other is a fish!

Q: What did the fish say when it hit a concrete wall?
A: 'Dam!'

Two drunken fishermen were staggering home up a dark country road. 'Hell Mike, we've stumbled into the graveyard and here's a stone of a man who lived to 103.'

'I'll be darned, Joe. Was it anyone we knew at all?'

'No, it's someone named Miles, from Sydney.'

'What's the biggest fish you ever caught?'

'That would be the one that measured 40 cm . . .'

'That's not so big!'

'Between the eyes?'

Q: Why are fish so smart?

A: Because they swim in schools!

A fisherman came home from an extended hospital stay to find his eight year old son riding a new ten speed bike.

'Boy,' he yelled, 'where did you get the money for that bike? It must have cost $600.'

'Dad, I earned it hiking. Every other night, while you were in the hospital, Mr Green from the bait shop came to see Ma. He'd give me $20 and tell me to go take a hike.'

Two guys go on a fishing trip.

They rent all the equipment: the reels, the rods, the wading suits, the rowboat, the car and even a cabin in the woods.

They spend a fortune.

The first day they go fishing they don't catch a thing.

The same thing happens on the second day and on the third day.

It goes on like this until finally, on the last day of their vacation, one of the men finally catches a fish.

As they're driving home they're really depressed.

One guy turns to the other and says, 'Do you realise that this one lousy fish we caught cost us fifteen hundred dollars?'

'Wow!' says the other guy 'It's a good job we didn't catch any more!'

Q: What do you call a deaf fishing boat captain?
A: Anything you like, he can't hear you.

QUICK THINKING

Susan, the barmaid at the local 'Fishermen's Watering Hole', was not the brightest of people, but she could make any drink without referring to the bar manual.

One day, she ran in and yelled to the owner, 'Fred, I just saw someone drive off in your new pickup.'

'Oh shit! Did you try to stop him?'

'No', she said, 'I did better than that. I got the licence number.'

Q: What is the definition of a 'Fisherman's Thumb'?
A: A temporary hook holder.

Q: What is the definition of a 'Fisherman's Knot'?
A: The insecure connection between your fly hook and your fishing line.

Q: What is the definition of a 'live bait'?
A: The biggest fish you will handle all day.

Q: What is the definition of a 'Treble Hook'?
A: A hook that trebles the odds of catching a fish but quadruples the odds of getting it caught in your thumb.

Q: What is the definition of a fisherman?
A: An obsessive individual who owns a house that is falling down due to neglect.

After a day on the water, John was coming home with his catch in a large bucket, his big tackle box and his pet parrot on his shoulder.

He was asked by a pretty young woman how to get to a particular address.

John said, 'It's at the other end of this alley. C'mon with me, I'm going that way.'

The young woman said, 'How do I know that when we get in that alley you won't hold me up against the wall, lift my skirt and ravish me?'

John said, 'With all I'm carrying? How could I possibly do that?'

The young woman said, 'Put the parrot down, put the bucket over the parrot, the tackle box on top of the bucket and I'll hold the fish.'

Q: Where do fish keep their money?
A: In the river bank.

'I caught a twenty pound salmon last week.'

'Were there any witnesses?'

'There sure were. If there hadn't been, it would have been forty pounds.'

Heard the one about the three blondes that went ice fishing and didn't catch anything?

By the time they cut a hole big enough for the boat to fit in it was time to go home.

A priest was walking along the cliffs at Dover when he came upon two locals pulling another man ashore on the end of a rope.

'That's what I like to see,' said the priest, 'A man helping his fellow man.'

As he was walking away, one local remarked to the other, 'Well, he sure doesn't know the first thing about shark fishing.'

There was a salmon fisherman who was out in the ocean fishing when his boat sank. He was lucky enough to make it to a deserted island where he had to survive on what he could find.

When the Coastguard eventually found him, the leader noticed there was a fire pit with the feathers of a protected bird all around.

He went over to the fisherman and said, 'You know, it's illegal to kill a California Condor, I'm afraid I'm going to have to arrest you.'

The fisherman protested for some time saying that he killed it because he was going to starve but eventually he calmed down.

'Out of curiosity,' the coastguard asked, 'What did it taste like?'

The fisherman replied, 'Well, it was kind of a mix between a Snowy Owl and a Bald Headed Eagle . . .'

Three blondes are sitting by the side of a river holding fishing poles with the lines in the water. A Game Warden comes up behind them, taps them on the shoulder and says, 'Excuse me, ladies, I'd like to see your fishing licences.'

'We don't have any,' replied the first blonde.

'Well, if you're going to fish, you need fishing licences,' said the Game Warden.

'But officer,' replied the second blonde, 'we aren't fishing. All we have are magnets at the end of our lines and we're collecting debris off the bottom of the river.'

The Game Warden lifted up all the lines and, sure enough, there were horseshoe magnets tied on the end of each line.

'Well, I know of no law against it,' said the Game Warden, 'take all the debris you want.'

And with that, the Game Warden left.

As soon as the Game Warden was out of sight, the three blondes started laughing hysterically.

'What a dumb Fish Cop,' the second blonde said to the other two, 'doesn't he know that there are steelhead in this river?!'

Once there was a boy named Odd.

He was the butt of jokes his whole life, because of his name.

Eventually he grew up to be a very successful fisherman and owner of three fish processing plants.

When Odd was about to die, he said, 'People have been teasing me my whole life and I don't want them doing that after I'm dead, so don't put my name on my gravestone.'

After Odd died, people saw his blank tombstone and said, 'That's odd.'

Jim had an awful day fishing on the lake, sitting in the blazing sun all day without catching a single one.

On his way home, he stopped at the supermarket and ordered four catfish.

He told the fish salesman, 'Pick four large ones out and throw them at me, will you?'

'Why do you want me to throw them at you?'

'Because I want to tell my wife that I caught them.'

'Okay, but I suggest that you take the orange roughy.'

'Why's that?'

'Because your wife came in earlier today and said that if you came by, I should tell you to take orange roughy. That's what she'd like for supper tonight.'

I HEAR VOICES

An eighty year old man was out fishing one day when he heard a voice.

Knowing no one was around he just thought he was hearing things.

Once again he heard, 'Psst . . . psst, hey you!'

The man looked around and saw a frog in the water.

He said to the frog, 'Are you talking to me?'

The frog answered, 'Yes, pick me up.'

So the man picked the frog up.

'Now kiss me and I will turn into the most beautiful woman you have ever seen.'

The man proceeded to put the frog in his coat pocket.

Pretty soon the man hears the frog's muffled voice again.

He reaches into his pocket and retrieves the frog.

'Hey, didn't you hear me? I said kiss me and I will turn into the most beautiful woman you have ever seen!'

'No thanks,' said the man, 'At my age I would rather have a talking frog.'

No one in this town could catch any fish except this one man.

The game warden asked him how he did it, so the man told the game warden that he would take him fishing the next day.

Once they got to the middle of the lake the man took out a stick of dynamite, lit it and threw it in the water.

After the explosion fish started floating to the top of the water.

The man took out a net and started picking up the fish.

The game warden told him that this was illegal.

The man took out another stick of dynamite and lit it.

He then handed it to the game warden and said, 'Are you going to fish or talk?'

One Saturday morning he gets up early, dresses quietly, gets his lunch made, puts on his long johns, grabs his dog and goes to the garage to hook up his boat to the truck and down to the driveway he goes . . .

When he comes out of his garage, the rain is pouring down. There is snow and sleet mixed in with the rain.

The wind is blowing at over 50mph.

Minutes later he returns to the garage.

He comes back into the house.

Turns the TV to the weather channel and he finds it is going to be very bad weather all day long, so he puts his boat back in the garage, quietly undresses and slips back into bed.

There he cuddles up to his wife's back, now anticipating something different and whispers, 'The weather out there is terrible'.

To which she sleepily replies, 'Yeah, can you believe my stupid husband is out fishing in it?'

Q: What did the fisherman that had sunglasses on say to the fish on the roof of his car?

A: Nothing because he didn't recognise him.

The first mate turns to the skipper and asks, 'Do you think we'll catch any fish today?'

The skipper replies, 'Cod willing.'

Two Norwegian anglers were being swept rapidly out to sea, clinging to the keel of their upturned boat, faces lashed by hail and sleet, bodies soaked by spray and icy waves.

Gunnar yelled to Leif, 'Turned out to be a rotten day, didn't it!'

Leif considered this point for a few seconds, then yelled back, 'Ja! Gunnar. Good job we decided not to go mountaineering!'

Two guys are talking about fishing.

One says to the other, 'I am NEVER going to take my wife fishing with me, ever again!'

'That bad, huh?'

'She did everything wrong! She talked too much, made the boat rock constantly, tried to stand up in the boat, baited the hook wrong, used the wrong lures and worst of all she caught more friggin' fish than I did!'

There are two kinds of fishermen. Those that fish for sport and those that catch something.

'How was the fishing today, Adrian?' asked his friend Stan back at the marina.

'Not very good. I only got fifty bites—one small fish and forty-nine mosquitoes.'

Q: Why does a fish take the bait in his mouth?
A: Because he doesn't have any hands.

Q: Why do they cut the heads off sardines?
A: So they don't bite each other in the can.

'I'm going fishing,' really means, 'I'm going to drink myself silly, get sun burnt and stand by a river with a stick in my hand, while the fish swim by in complete safety.'

EXCUSES!

The manager of a small business and his secretary decide to go over to her place for some 'gymnastics'. Afterwards, they both fall asleep.

When the manager wakes up and looks at his watch, he discovers that it is after eight o'clock in the evening.

He jumps up in a panic, wondering what he's going to say to his wife.

He tells the secretary to quickly take his shoes out into the yard and rub them around in the grass.

Then he finishes dressing and goes home.

When the man opens the door to the house, his wife is standing in the doorway fuming and asks him where the hell he's been until 8.30 in the evening.

The man calmly replies that he and his secretary are having an affair and that they had fallen asleep after going to her place this afternoon.

His wife looked at him very carefully and when she saw the state of his shoes, she exclaimed: 'You liar, you've been fishing!'

A small town doctor was famous in the area for always catching large fish.

One day while he was on one of his frequent fishing trips he got a call that a woman at a neighbouring farm was giving birth.

He rushed to her aid and delivered a healthy baby boy.

The farmer had nothing to weigh the baby with so the doctor used his fishing scales.

The baby weighed 22 lbs 10 oz.

Three fishermen were fishing when they came upon a mermaid.

The mermaid offered them one wish each.

The first fisherman said: 'Double my IQ,' so the mermaid did it and to his surprise he started reciting Shakespeare.

The second fisherman said, 'Triple my IQ.'

Sure enough, the mermaid did it and amazingly he started doing math problems he didn't know existed.

The third fisherman was so impressed he asked the mermaid to quadruple his IQ.

The mermaid said, 'Are you sure about this? It will change your whole life!'

The fisherman said, 'Yes, go ahead.'

The mermaid turned him into a woman . . .

Two blondes rented a fishing boat and were having a great day catching fish.

The first blonde said, 'This is such a great spot, we need to mark it so we can come back.'

The second blonde proceeded to put a mark on the side of the boat.

The first blonde asked, 'What are you doing?'

The second blonde replied, 'Marking the spot.'

'Don't be stupid,' the first blonde said. 'What if we don't get the same boat next time?'

Two Irishmen were walking down the street with two salmons each under their arms.

Two other Irishmen, who were walking in the opposite direction, see the two lucky fishermen and ask, 'How did you catch those?'

'Well it's like this!' says one, 'Michael here holds my legs over the bridge and I grab the salmon as they swim up the river. We got four salmon. A great day's fishing!'

So the fishless pair looks at each other and agrees to give it a try.

They get to the bridge and Sean calls to his friend, 'Hold my legs now, Paddy.'

After he has been hanging there upside down for thirty minutes he cries, 'Pull me up! Pull me up!'

Paddy asks, 'Do you have a fish Sean?'

'No,' replies Sean, 'there's a bloody train coming!'

ARE YOU A GENIE?

A man was surf fishing along the beach when he found a bottle.

He looked around but didn't see anyone so he opened it.

A genie appeared and thanked the man for letting him out.

The genie said, 'I am so grateful to get out of that bottle that I will grant you any wish, but I can only grant one.'

The man thought for a while and finally said, 'I have always wanted to go to Hawaii and fish along the beautiful beaches of Hawaii. I've never been able to go because I cannot fly. Airplanes are much too frightening for me. On a boat, I see all that water and I become very claustrophobic. So I wish for a road to be built from here to Hawaii.'

The genie thought for a few minutes and finally said, 'No, I don't think I can do that. Just think of all the work involved. Consider all the piling needed to hold up a highway and how deep they would have to go to reach the bottom of the ocean. Imagine the amount of pavement needed. No, that really is just too much to ask.'

The man thought for a few minutes and then told the genie, 'There is one other thing I have always wanted. I would like to be able to understand women. What makes them laugh and cry, why are they temperamental, why are they so difficult to get along with, when they want attention, when they don't. Basically, what makes them tick.'

The genie thought for a while and said, 'So, do you want two lanes or four?'

A couple goes on vacation to a fishing resort in northern Minnesota.

The husband likes to fish at the crack of dawn.

The wife likes to read.

One morning the husband returns after several hours of fishing and decides to take a short nap.

Although she isn't familiar with the lake, the wife decides to take the boat.

She motors out a short distance, anchors and continues to read her book.

Along comes the game warden in his boat.

He pulls up alongside her and says, 'Good morning, Ma'am, what are you doing?'

'Reading my book,' she replies, thinking to herself, 'Isn't that obvious?'

'You're in a restricted fishing area,' he informs her.

'But officer, I'm not fishing. Can't you see that?'

'Yes, but you have all the equipment. I'll have to take you in and write you up.'

'If you do that, I'll have to charge you with rape,' says the woman.

'But I haven't even touched you,' says the game warden.

'That's true, but you do have all the equipment.'

The moral of this story is to never argue with a woman who reads.

A woman goes into a shop to buy a rod and reel as a gift. She doesn't know which one to get so she just grabs one and goes over to the counter where there's a shop assistant wearing dark shades.

'Excuse me sir,' she says, 'can you tell me anything about this rod and reel?'

The assistant replies, 'Ma'am I'm blind but if you drop it

on the counter I can tell you everything you need to know about it from the sound it makes.'

She didn't believe him, but dropped it on the counter anyway.

He said, 'That's a six inch graphite rod with a Zebco 202 reel and ten pound test line. It's a good all around rod and reel and it's only $20.00.'

The lady said, 'It's amazing that you can tell all that just by the sound of it dropping on the counter. I think it's what I'm looking for, so I'll take it.'

He walks behind the counter to the register and in the meantime the woman breaks wind big-time.

At first she is embarrassed, but then realises that there is no way he could tell it was her as being blind he wouldn't know that she was the only person around.

The assistant rings up the sale and says, 'That will be $25.50.'

She says, 'But didn't you say it was $20.00?'

'Yes ma'am, the rod and reel is $20.00, but the duck call is $3.00 and the catfish stink bait is $2.50.'

One day, two guys Joe and Bob were out fishing.

A funeral service passes over the bridge they're fishing by and Bob takes off his hat and puts it over his heart.

He does this until the funeral service passes by.

Joe then says, 'Gee Bob, I didn't know you had it in you!'

Bob then replies, 'It's the least I could do. After all I was married to her for 30 years.'

Sven was going for his morning walk one day when he walked past Ole's house and saw a sign that said 'Boat For Sale'.

This confused Sven because he knew that Ole didn't own a boat, so he finally decided to go in and ask Ole about it.

'Hey Ole,' said Sven, 'I noticed da sign in your yard dat says 'Boat For Sale,' but ya ain't ever been fishun and don't even have a boat. All ya have is your old John Deere tractor and combine harvester.'

Ole calmly replied, 'Yup and they're boat for sale.'

Two boys were sitting on the river's edge fishing. One turns to the other and says, 'Do fish grow fast?'

The other boy replies, 'I think so. Every time my Dad tells the story about the one that got away it grows another few inches.'

First person:	Don't fish in this sea. I went in too far and a shark just bit off my foot!
Second person:	Which one?
First person:	I don't know. All sharks look the same to me.

Mummy why can't I go swimming in the sea?
Because there are sharks in the sea.
But Mummy, Daddy is swimming in the sea.
That's different—he is insured.

Mother: Have you given the goldfish fresh water today?
Son: No, they haven't finished the water I gave them yesterday.

'Little boy, what are you fishing for?'
'I'm not fishing, I'm drowning worms.'

One recent Sunday, a young boy arrived to his Sunday school class late.

His teacher knew that the boy was usually very prompt and asked him if anything was wrong.

The boy replied no, that he was going to go fishing, but that his dad told him that he needed to go to church instead.

The teacher was very impressed and asked the boy if his father had explained to him why it was more important to go to church rather than to go fishing.

To which the boy replied, 'Yes, ma'am, he did. My dad said that he didn't have enough bait for both of us.'

CLEVER, CLEVER!

Four married guys go fishing.

After an hour, the following conversation took place.

First guy: 'You have no idea what I had to do to be able to come out fishing this weekend. I had to promise my wife that I will paint every room in the house next weekend.'

Second guy: 'That's nothing; I had to promise my wife that I will build her a new deck for the pool.'

Third guy: 'Man, you both have it easy! I had to promise my wife that I will remodel the kitchen for her.'

They continue to fish when they realized that the fourth guy has not said a word. So they asked him, 'You haven't said anything about what you had to do to be able to come fishing this weekend. What's the deal?'

The fourth guy said: 'I just set my alarm for 5.30 am. When it went off, I shut off my alarm, gave the wife a nudge and said, 'Fishing or sex?' and she said, 'Don't forget your sweater . . .'

Man: Can I have a fly rod and reel for my son?

Fishing Shop Owner: Sorry sir we don't do trades.

What did the mummy sardine say to her children when they saw a submarine?

Don't worry; it's only a tin of people.

A man went fishing one day.

He looked over the side of his boat and saw a snake with a frog in its mouth.

Feeling sorry for the frog, he reached down, gently took the frog from the snake and set the frog free.

But then he felt sorry for the snake.

He looked around the boat, but he had no food.

All he had was a bottle of bourbon.

So he opened the bottle and gave the snake a few shots.

The snake went off happy, the frog was happy and the man was happy to have performed such good deeds.

He thought everything was great until about ten minutes passed and he heard something knock against the side of the boat.

In stunned disbelief, the fisherman looked down and saw the snake was back with two other frogs!

FISHY RIDDLES

Q: What is the best way of stopping a fish from smelling?
A: Cut off his nose.

Q: What happened to the fishing boat that sank in piranha fish infested waters?
A: It came back with a skeleton crew.

Q: What whizzes along a riverbed on three wheels?
A: A motor-Pike and a side-Carp.

Q: Where do fish wash?
A: In a river basin.

Q: Two fathers and two sons went fishing—how many people were there?
A: Three, they were all members of the same family—grandfather, father, son.

Q: Where do whales get weighed?
A: At a whale weigh station.

Q: What kind of fish do you find in a bird cage?
A: A perch.

Q: What is the best way to communicate with a fish?
A: Drop it a line.

Q: Where do fish keep their money?
A: In the river bank.

Q: What is the best fish on ice?
A: A skate.

Q: Why did the trout cross the road?
A: Because it was the chicken's day off.

Q: What fish are musical?
A: Tuna fish.

Q: If fish lived on land, which country would they live in?
A: Finland.

Q: What did one rock pool say to the other rock pool?
A: Show me your mussels you big wanker.

Q: How do you kiss a pike?
A: Very carefully.

Q: Why do they call him 'Fish'?
A: Because he cannot keep his mouth shut.

Q: When I'm fishing on a river bank, how do I avoid infection from biting insects?
A: That's easy—don't bite them.

Q: What is the wettest animal in the world?
A: A reindeer.

Q: What sits at the bottom of the sea and shivers?
A: A nervous wreck.

Q: What has big sharp teeth, a tail, scales and a trunk?
A: A pike going on holiday.

Q: What is the fastest fish in the sea?
A: Go-carp.

Q: Why did the salmon cross the road?
A: Because it was tied to the chicken.

Q: What did the boy octopus sing to the girl octopus?
A: I want to hold your hand, hand, hand, hand, hand, hand, hand, hand.

Q: What do you get if you cross a whale with a computer?
A: A four tonne know it all.

Q: Why do they call him 'River'?
A: Because the biggest part of him is his mouth.

Q: What do you get if you cross a rose with a pike?
A: I don't know but I wouldn't put my nose too close to smell it.

Q: Where do you find a crab with no legs?
A: Exactly where you left it.

Q: What is yellow and dangerous?
A: Pike infested custard.

Q: What do you call a deaf pike.
A: Anything you like, he cannot hear you.

CHEERS!

FISHERMAN'S GUIDE TO TOO MUCH BEER DRINKING AND ITS CURES

SYMPTOM: Feet cold and wet.
FAULT: Glass being held at incorrect angle.
ACTION: Rotate glass so that open end points towards ceiling.

SYMPTOM: Feet warm and wet.
FAULT: Improper bladder control.
ACTION: Stand next to nearest dog, complain about house training.

SYMPTOM: Beer unusually pale and tasteless.
FAULT: Glass empty.
ACTION: Get someone to buy you another beer.

SYMPTOM: Opposite wall covered with fluorescent lights.
FAULT: You have fallen over backward.
ACTION: Have yourself leashed to bar.

SYMPTOM: Mouth contains cigarette butts.
FAULT: You have fallen forward.
ACTION: See above.

SYMPTOM: Beer tasteless, front of your shirt is wet.
FAULT: Mouth not open or glass applied to wrong part of face.
ACTION: Retire to restroom, practise in mirror.

SYMPTOM: Floor blurred.
FAULT: You are looking through bottom of empty glass.
ACTION: Get someone to buy you another beer.

SYMPTOM: Floor moving.
FAULT: You are being carried out.
ACTION: Find out if you are being taken to another bar.

SYMPTOM: Room seems unusually dark.
FAULT: Bar has closed.
ACTION: Confirm home address with bartender.

SYMPTOM: Taxi suddenly takes on colourful aspect and textures.
FAULT: Beer consumption has exceeded personal limitations.
ACTION: Cover mouth.

SYMPTOM: Everyone looks up to you and smiles.
FAULT: You are dancing on the table.
ACTION: Fall on somebody cushy-looking.

SYMPTOM: Beer is crystal-clear.
FAULT: It's water. Somebody is trying to sober you up.
ACTION: Punch him.

SYMPTOM: Hands hurt, nose hurts, mind unusually clear.
FAULT: You have been in a fight.
ACTION: Apologise to everyone you see, just in case it was them.

SYMPTOM: Don't recognise anyone, don't recognise the room you're in.
FAULT: You've wandered into the wrong party.
ACTION: See if they have free beer.

SYMPTOM: Your singing sounds distorted.
FAULT: The beer is too weak.
ACTION: Have more beer until your voice improves.

SYMPTOM: Don't remember the words to the song.
FAULT: Beer is just right.
ACTION: Play air guitar.

FISHERMEN AND THE DRINK

An old fisherman staggered home late after another evening with his drinking buddies.

Shoes in left hand to avoid waking his wife, he tiptoed as quietly as he could towards the stairs leading to their upstairs bedroom, but misjudged the bottom step in the darkened entryway.

As he caught himself by grabbing the banister, his body swung around and he landed heavily on his rump. A whiskey bottle in each back pocket broke and made the landing especially painful.

Managing to suppress a yelp, he sprung up, pulled down his pants and examined his lacerated and bleeding cheeks in a mirror of a nearby darkened hallway, then managed to find a large full box of band-aids before proceeding to place a patch as best he could on each place he saw blood.

After hiding the now almost empty box, he managed to shuffle and stumble his way to bed.

In the morning, he awakens with screaming pain in his head and butt and sees his wife staring at him from across the room. He hears her say: 'You were drunk again last night!'

Forcing himself to ignore his agony, he looked meekly at her and replied: 'Now, honey, why would you say such a mean thing?'

'Well,' she said, 'there is the front door left open, the glass at the bottom of the stairs, the drops of blood trailing through the house and your bloodshot eyes but, mostly . . . there are band-aids stuck on the downstairs mirror!'

A drunken fisherman waddled out of the pub and stumbled upon a traditional baptismal service at the river where he fished.

He walked out in the water to where the minister stood.

The minister turned to the drunk and said, 'Mister, are you ready to find Jesus?'

The drunk looks at the preacher and says, 'Yes, Rev, I sure am.'

The minister then dunks the fellow under the water, pulls him up asking, 'Have you found Jesus?'

The drunk replies, 'No.'

So the preacher dunks him a bit longer, pulls him up and again asks, 'Did you find Jesus?'

The drunk replies, 'No.'

The minister gets disgusted, pushes the man under the water for about 30 seconds, pulls him up and asks in a harsh voice, 'Now, my good man, have you found Jesus yet?'

The old fisherman wipes his eyes, spits out water and says to the minister, 'No! Are you sure this is where he fell in?'

One day a rather inebriated ice fisherman drilled a hole in the ice and peered into the hole and a loud voice said, 'There are no fish down there.'

He walked several yards away and drilled another hole and peered into the hole and again the voice said, 'There's no fish down there.'

He then walked about 50 yards away and drilled another hole and again the voice said, 'There's no fish down there.'

He looked up into the sky and asked, 'God, is that you?'

'No, you idiot,' the voice said, 'it's the rink manager.'

A fisherman stumbles into the Yacht Club bar, approaches the only customer there and says, 'Hi, my name is Alby, could I buy you a drink?'

'Why of course', came the reply, 'and my name is Paul.'

The introductions over, the question arose as to where Alby was from.

He said, 'I'm from Bainbridge, Georgia. I went to Bainbridge High and graduated in 1962.'

Paul was stunned for a moment, but said, 'I don't believe this. I went to Bainbridge High and I graduated in 1962.'

At this time, another customer came into the bar, sat down and asked the bartender, 'What's up?'

The bartender shook his head and said, 'Not much. The Brown twins are drunk again.'

HANDY PHRASES

FISHING BAR PHRASES AND WHAT THEY MEAN

'You get this one, next round is on me.'
[We won't be here long enough to get another round.]

'I'll get this one, next round is on you.'
[Happy hour is about to end . . . beers are a dollar now, but by the next round they'll be $4.50 a pop, sucker.]

'Hey, where is that friend of yours?'
[I have no interest in talking to you, but I want to get your attractive friend in a compromising position.]

'What do you have on tap?'
[What's cheap?]

'I'll have a glass of house white.' (Female)
[I'm easy.]

'I'll have a glass of house white.' (Male)
[I'm gay.]

'I'll have an amaretto and OJ.' (Female)
[I'm really easy.]

'I'll have an amaretto and OJ.' (Male)
[I'm really gay.]

'Ever try a body shot?' (Female to Male)
[If this is how wild I am in the bar, can you imagine what I'll do to you in bed?]

'I don't feel well, let's go home.' (Female)
[You're paying more attention to your friends than to me.]

'I don't feel well, let's go home.' (Male)
[I'm horny.]

'Excuse me.' (Male to Male)
[Get the hell out of the way.]

'Excuse me.' (Male to Female)
[I am going to grope you now and blame it on the crowd.]

'Excuse me.' (Female to Male)
[Don't even think about groping me, just get the hell out of my way.]

An Englishman, a Scotsman and an Irishman had been fishing and, at the end of the day they walked into a pub together.

They each proceeded to buy a pint of Guinness.

Just as they were about to enjoy their creamy beverage, a fly landed in each of their pints and became stuck in the thick head.

The Englishman pushed his beer from him in disgust.

The Scotsman fished the offending fly out of his beer and continued drinking it as if nothing had happened.

The Irishman picked the fly out of his drink, held it out over the beer and yelled, 'Spit it out! Give it back to me, you bastard!'

Why every good fisherman should enjoy a few beers: 'Sometimes when I reflect back on all the beer I drink, I feel ashamed. Then I look into the glass and think about the workers in the brewery and all of their hopes and dreams. If I didn't drink this beer, they might be out of work and their dreams would be shattered. Then I say to myself, 'It is better that I drink this beer and let their dreams come true than be selfish and worry about my liver.'

Jack Handy

'I feel sorry for people who don't drink. When they wake up in the morning, that's as good as they're going to feel all day.'

Frank Sinatra

'An intelligent man is sometimes forced to be drunk to spend time with his fools.'

Ernest Hemingway

'When I read about the evils of drinking, I gave up reading.'

Henny Youngman

'24 hours in a day, 24 beers in a case. Coincidence? I think not.'

Stephen Wright

'When we drink, we get drunk. When we get drunk, we fall asleep. When we fall asleep, we commit no sin. When we commit no sin, we go to heaven. So, let's all get drunk and go to heaven!'

Brian O'Rourke

'Beer is proof that God loves us and wants us to be happy.'

Benjamin Franklin

'Without question, the greatest invention in the history of mankind is beer. Oh, I grant you that the wheel was also a fine invention, but the wheel does not go nearly as well with pizza.'

Dave Barry

'To some it's a six-pack, to me it's a Support Group. Salvation in a can!'

Thomas Blackburn

'A psychologist once said that we know little about the conscience except that it is soluble in alcohol.'

THE BUFFALO THEORY

A herd of buffalo can only move as fast as the slowest buffalo.

And when the herd is hunted, the slowest and weakest animals at the back are killed first. This natural selection is good for the herd as a whole, because the general speed and health of the whole group keeps improving by the regular killing of the weakest members.

In much the same way, the human brain can only operate as fast as the slowest brain cells.

Excessive intake of alcohol, as we know, kills brain cells.

But naturally, it attacks the slowest and weakest brain cells first.

In this way, regular consumption of beer eliminates the weaker brain cells, making the brain a faster and more efficient machine.

That's why you always feel smarter after a few beers.

IT'S HOW YOU SAY IT

A fisherman, who had been out on the boat, fishing and drinking an ale or two, sat down on a subway seat next to a priest.

His tie was stained, he smelled of bait and a half empty bottle of gin was sticking out of his torn coat pocket.

He opened his newspaper and began reading.

After a few minutes, the man turned to the priest and asked, 'Say, Father, what causes arthritis?'

'My son, it is caused by loose living, being with cheap, wicked women, too much alcohol and contempt for your fellow man.'

'Well, I'll be damned,' the drunk muttered, returning to his paper.

The priest, thinking about what he had said, nudged the man and apologised. 'I'm very sorry. I didn't mean to come on so strong. How long have you had arthritis?'

'I don't have it, Father. I was just reading here that the Pope does.'

A group of friends are on a fishing trip and spend the night in a small country pub. After dinner they go into the bar.

As they are sitting there drinking their beers, someone stands up and shouts, '27!' and the entire bar bursts into hysterical laughter.

A few moments later, someone else stands up and yells, '16!' Once again, the entire bar bursts into fits of laughter.

Soon, a third man stands up and shouts, 'Six!' Again, everyone in the bar laughs.

The completely confused strangers walk up to the bartender and ask what all the laughing is about.

The bartender replies, 'See, we're such a small town that everyone knows everyone and all of their jokes. So to make life easier we catalogued all of our jokes. Now instead of telling the whole joke, we just shout out its number and everyone knows what joke its and we laugh.'

The fishermen nod in agreement and sits down.

After a few more people stand up and shout numbers, one of them decides he wants to join in.

He stands up and shouts, '17!'

Nobody laughs.

The bartender shakes his head and says, 'Man, you just didn't tell it right . . .'

A preacher was having a heart-to-heart talk with a rootin', tootin', shootin' member of his flock, whose drinking of moonshine invariably led to quarrelling with his neighbours and occasional shotgun blasts at some of them.

'Can't you see, Ben,' intoned the parson, 'That not one good thing comes out of this drinking?'

'Well, I sort of disagree there,' replied the backslider. 'It makes me miss the folks I shoot at.'

WARNING—DON'T DRINK THAT!

Next time you are out on the boat, you might just find a warning like this one about that next can of beer you are about to open:

WARNING: Consumption of alcohol may cause obstruct the time-space continuum. Small and sometimes large, gaps of time may disappear from your memory bank.

WARNING: Consumption of alcohol may cause the description of the fish you caught to be considerably enhanced, thus causing uneasy feelings of disbelief amongst listeners.

WARNING: Consumption of alcohol may cause you to tell the same boring story over and over again until your friends want to smash your head in.

WARNING: Consumption of alcohol may make you think you are whispering when you are actually shouting loudly.

WARNING: Consumption of alcohol may create the illusion that you are tougher, more handsome, smarter, talk better and fight harder than a really, really, really big biker named 'Killer McKenzie'.

WARNING: Consumption of alcohol may cause you to tell the Managing Director what you really think about him and his crappy little company while photocopying your bum at the staff Christmas Party.

WARNING: Consumption of alcohol can make you dance like a jerk.

WARNING: Consumption of alcohol may lead you to believe that ex-girlfriends are really dying for you to telephone them at four o'clock in the morning.

WARNING: Consumption of alcohol may cause you to thay things like thish.

WARNING: Consumption of alcohol may leave you wondering what the hell ever happened to your pants anyway.

WARNING: Consumption of alcohol may cause you to roll over in the morning and see something really scary.

WARNING: Consumption of alcohol is the leading cause of inexplicable rug burn on the forehead.

WARNING: Consumption of alcohol may lead you to believe you are invisible.

WARNING: Consumption of alcohol may lead you to think people are laughing *with* you.

WARNING: Consumption of alcohol may make you think you can logically converse with other members of the opposite sex without spitting.

FISHERMEN AND RELATIONSHIPS

A FISHERMAN'S EXPERIENCE WITH THE OPPOSITE SEX

When I was 14, I hoped that one day I would have a girlfriend.

When I was 16 I got a girlfriend, but there was no passion. So I decided I needed a passionate girl with a zest for life.

In college I dated a passionate girl, but she was too emotional. Everything was an emergency; she was a drama queen, cried all the time and threatened suicide. So I decided I needed a girl with stability.

When I was 25 I found a very stable girl but she was boring. She was totally predictable and never got excited about anything. Life became so dull that I decided that I needed a girl with some excitement.

When I was 28 I found an exciting girl, but I couldn't keep up with her. She rushed from one thing to another, never settling on anything. She did mad impetuous things and made me miserable as often as happy. She was great fun initially and very energetic, but directionless. So I decided to find a girl with some real ambition.

When I turned 31, I found a smart ambitious girl with her feet planted firmly on the ground and married her. She was so ambitious that she divorced me and took everything I owned.

I am now 40 and am looking for a girl with very big

warm tits who will have the bed warm when I come in from fishing.

A policeman is walking his beat when he finds a totally drunk fisherman collapsed against a building, weeping uncontrollably and holding his car keys in his hands. He is moaning something about, 'They took my car!'

Seeing he is quite well dressed, the cop thinks he may have a real case of theft on his hands and proceeds to question the man.

'What are your car keys doing out?'

'My car, it was right on the end of my key and those bastards stole it! Please ossifer, get my Porsche back. My God, it was right on the end of my key! Where is it? They stole it and it was right here; right on my key!'

'Okay, okay, stand up, let's get some more information,' says the officer.

He stands the man up and notices his penis is hanging out.

'Goddamn, mister, your dick is hanging out, would you put that thing away!'

The man looks down, sees his prick hanging there and screams, 'Oh my God, they stole my girlfriend, too!'

MEN! VIVA LA DIFFERENCE!

1. A man will pay $2 for a $1 item he wants, a woman will pay $1 for a $2 item that she doesn't want.
2. A woman worries about the future until she gets a husband. A man never worries about the future until he gets a wife.
3. A successful man is one who makes more money than

his wife can spend. A successful woman is one who can find such a man.

4. To be happy with a man you must understand him a lot and love him a little. To be happy with a woman you must love her a lot and not try to understand her at all.
5. Married men love longer than single men—but married men are a lot more willing to die.
6. Any married man should forget his mistakes—there's no use in two people remembering the same thing.
7. Men wake up as good-looking as they went to bed. Women somehow deteriorate during the night.

8. A woman marries a man expecting he will change, but he doesn't. A man marries a woman expecting that she won't change and she does.
9. A woman has the last word in any argument. Anything a man says after that is the beginning of a new argument.
10. There are two times when a man doesn't understand a woman—before marriage and after marriage.

Married men revealed that they do this twice as often as single men: change their underwear.

HOW BIG?

FISHERMEN'S PENIS

The only thing that the Australian Taxation Department has not taxed yet is the male penis. This is due to the fact that 40% of the time it is hanging around unemployed,

30% of the time it is hard up,

20% of the time it is pissed off,

10% of the time it is in the hole.

On top of that, it has two dependents and they are both nuts.

The penis will soon be taxed according to size:

10–12 inch	Luxury Tax $30.00
8–10 inch	Pole Tax $25.00
5–8 inch	Privilege Tax $15.00
4–5 inch	Nuisance Tax $3.00.

Males exceeding 12 inches must file under Capital Gains.

Anyone who measures under 4 inches is eligible for a refund.

PLEASE DO NOT ASK FOR AN EXTENSION!

As of next week Viagra will only be available through the chemists by its chemical name.

So please ask for MYCOXAFLOPPIN, thank you.

SEMINARS FOR FISHERMEN

- You Can Do the Housework, Too.

- Understanding the Female Response to You Coming In Drunk at 4 am.
- Wonderful Laundry Techniques (formerly called Don't Wash My Silks).
- Parenting—Participation Doesn't End With Conception.
- Get A Life—Learn To Cook.

ARE YOU A NEANDERTHAL FISHERMAN?

1. Do your eyebrows meet in the middle?
2. Can you lock your knees in an upright position?
3. Got a chin?
4. How about a forehead?
5. Do you ever open beer bottles with your teeth?
6. Pigeon-toed?
7. Is your nickname 'Duke', 'Butch' or 'Animal'?

ZZzzzzzzzz

Q: Why do fishermen snore?
A: Because their balls hang over their arses and they vapour lock.

Did you hear that the first consignment of Viagra to be imported into Britain was nicked?

Police are looking for hardened criminals in possession of swollen goods.

WHAT FISHERMEN ARE REALLY THINKING WHEN THEY SAY THE THINGS THEY DO:

'It's a guy thing.'
[There is no rational thought pattern connected with it and you have no chance at all of making it logical.]

'Sure, honey,' or 'Yes, dear.'
[Absolutely nothing. It's a conditioned response like Pavlov's dog drooling.]

'My wife doesn't understand me.'
[She's heard all my stories before and is tired of them.]

'It would take too long to explain.'
[I have no idea how it works.]

'I'm getting more exercise lately.'
[The batteries in the remote are dead.]

'Take a break, honey, you're working too hard.'
[I can't hear the game over the vacuum cleaner.]

'That's interesting, dear.'
[Are you still talking?]

'You expect too much of me.'
[You want me to stay awake.]

'That's women's work.'
[It's difficult, dirty and thankless.]

'Will you marry me?'
[Both my roommates have moved out, I can't find the washer and there is no more peanut butter.]

'I do help around the house.'
[I once put a dirty towel in the laundry basket.]

'I can't find it.'
[It didn't fall into my outstretched hands, so I'm completely clueless.]

'What did I do this time?'
[What did you catch me at?]

'She's one of those rabid feminists.'
[She refused to make my coffee.]

'I'm going to stop off for a quick one with the guys.'
[I am planning on drinking myself into a vegetative stupor with my chest pounding, mouth breathing, pre-evolutionary companions.]

'You know I could never love anyone else.'
[I am used to the way you yell at me and realise it could be worse.]

'You look terrific.'
[Oh, God, please don't try on one more outfit. I'm starving.]

'I missed you.'
[I can't find my sock drawer, the kids are hungry and we are out of toilet paper.]

'I'm not lost. I know exactly where we are.'
[No one will ever see us alive again.]

'We share the housework.'
[I make the messes, she cleans them up.]

'This relationship is getting too serious.'
[I like you more than my truck.]

'I recycle.'
[We could pay the rent with the money from my empties.]

'I don't need to read the instructions.'
[I am perfectly capable of screwing it up without printed help.]

'I broke up with her.'
[She dumped me.]

A BLOKEY THING

THE MALE CHAUVINIST PIG IS ALIVE AND WELL AND FISHING EVERY SATURDAY

Q: What's worse than a male chauvinist pig?
A: A woman that won't do what she's told.

Q: What do you call a woman with two brain cells?
A: Pregnant.

Q: How many men does it take to open a beer?
A: None. It should be open by the time she brings it.

Q: Why is a Laundromat a really bad place to pick up a woman?
A: Because a woman who can't even afford a washing machine will never be able to support you.

Q: Why do women have smaller feet than men?
A: So they can stand closer to the kitchen sink.

Q: How do you know when a woman's about to say something smart?
A: She starts her sentence with 'A man once told me . . .'

Q: How do you fix a woman's watch?
A: You don't. There's a clock on the oven!

Q: Why do men pass gas more than women?
A: Because women won't shut up long enough to build up pressure.

Q: Why were shopping carts invented?
A: To teach women to walk on their hind legs.

Q: If your dog is barking at the back door and your wife is yelling at the front door, who do you let in first?
A: The dog, of course . . . at least he'll shut up after you let him in.

Q: Which food diminishes a woman's sex drive.
A: Wedding cake.

FISHERMEN'S JOKES ABOUT WOMEN

- I married Miss Right. I just didn't know her first name was Always.
- I haven't spoken to my wife for 18 months—I don't like to interrupt her.
- All wives are alike, but they have different faces so you can tell them apart.
- Women are like guns, keep one around long enough and you're going to want to shoot it.
- Bigamy is having one wife too many. Some say monogamy is the same.
- Marriage is a three ring circus: engagement ring, wedding ring and suffering.

SOUND ADVICE

HOW TO TALK ABOUT FISHERMEN AND STILL BE POLITICALLY CORRECT . . .

- He does not have a beer gut; he has developed a *liquid grain storage facility*.
- He is not quiet; he is a *conversational minimalist*.
- He is not stupid; he suffers from *minimal cranial development*.
- He does not get lost; he *discovers alternative destinations*.
- He is not balding; he is in *follicle regression*.
- He is not a cradle robber; he prefers *generational differential relationships*.
- He does not get falling-down drunk; he becomes *accidentally horizontal*.
- He does not act like a total ass; he develops a case of *rectal cranial inversion*.
- He is not short; he is *anatomically compact*.
- He does not constantly talk about cars; he has a *vehicular addiction*.
- He is not unsophisticated; he is *socially malformed*.
- He does not eat like a pig; he suffers from *reverse bulimia*.
- He does not hog the blankets; he is *thermally unappreciative*.
- He is not a male chauvinist pig; he has *swine empathy*.
- He doesn't have a dirty mind; he has *introspective pornographic moments*.

- He is not afraid of commitment; he is *monogamously challenged.*

One day Bill came home absolutely ashen.

His wife could see at once that something was seriously wrong.

'What's wrong, Bill?' she asked.

'Do you remember that I told you how I had this tremendous urge to put my penis in the pickle slicer?'

'Oh, Bill, you didn't.'

'Yes, I did.'

'My God, Bill, what happened?'

'I got fired.'

'No, Bill. I mean, what happened with the pickle-slicer?'

'Oh. She got fired too.'

A young fisherman and his older mate go down to the red light district of town.

The mate is betting every person he meets that his young friend can screw and satisfy one hundred women in a row, without pausing.

Bets are made and they agree that they'll meet the next day to complete the arrangement.

The next day, one hundred women are lined up and the young Romeo drops his pants and begins the task at hand.

True to his word, he moves from one to the next, satisfying each one without pausing: 1 . . . 2 . . . 3 . . . on and on he goes: 49 . . . 50 . . . 51 . . . He slows down somewhat: 83 . . . 84 . . . 85 . . . but he is still moving from one to the next and the women are still satisfied: 97 . . . 98 . . . 99 . . .

Before he can get to the last woman he has a heart attack and dies.

His mate scratches his head and says, 'I don't understand it! It went perfectly at practice this morning!'

WHY FISHING MATES ARE BETTER THAN WOMEN

- You can enjoy a fishing mate's company all month long.
- Fishing stains wash out.
- You don't have to wine and dine fishing mates.
- Your fishing mates will always wait patiently for you in the car while you play baseball.
- When your fishing mate gets boring, you come home.
- Hangovers go away.
- Fishing mates are never late.
- When you go to a bar, you know you can always pick up a fishing mate.
- Fishing mates never get a headache.
- After you've been fishing, you don't need to give the boat a cuddle.

- A fishing mate won't get upset if you have another fishing mate sometimes.
- You can catch more than one fish a night and not feel guilty.
- You can share a fishing mate with your friends.
- You always know you're the first one to catch a fish.
- Fishing mates don't demand equality.
- A fishing mate doesn't care when you come.
- If you change from fishing to another hobby you don't have to pay alimony.

A fisherman decided that it was time to teach his son how to say prayers.

After the kid had learned them well enough to say on his own, his Dad said he could choose someone special and ask for God's blessing for that person.

The first night the little boy said his prayers, he ended with, 'And God, please bless my puppy.'

However, the next morning the little dog ran out the door and was killed by a car.

That night the little kid asked God to bless his cat.

And, sure enough, the next morning the cat slipped out and took on the biggest dog in the neighbourhood and lost.

When the kid asked God to bless his goldfish, the fish was found floating upside down on the top.

That night the little kid ended with, 'God, please give an extra special blessing to my father.'

The father couldn't sleep. He couldn't eat breakfast in the morning. He was afraid to drive to work. He couldn't get any work done because he was petrified. He was going to go fishing that weekend, but he couldn't even think about it.

Finally quitting time came and he walked home, expecting to drop dead any minute.

When he arrived home, the house was a mess. His wife was lying on the couch still dressed in her robe. The dishes from breakfast were still on the table and the father was furious.

He yelled at his wife, telling her that he had had the worst day of his life and here she was, sitting in a mess and she hadn't even gotten dressed.

She looked at him and said, 'Shut up! My day was worse. The mailman had a heart attack on our front porch . . .!'

RIDDLE ME SOME MORE

Q: Why did the lobster blush?
A: It saw the Queen Mary's bottom.

Q: Why did the fish blush?
A: Because it saw the sea weed.

Q: What lives under the sea and carries a lot of people?
A: An octobus.

Q: What do sea monsters eat?
A: Fish and ships.

Q: What can fly under the water?
A: A bluebottle in a submarine.

Q: What has antlers and sucks your blood?
A: A moose-quito.

Q: Why are fish smarter than mice?
A: Because they live in schools.

Q: What fish terrorises other fish?
A: Jack the Kipper.

Q: What should you do if you find a shark in your bed?
A: Sleep somewhere else.

Q: What do you call a pike with a gun?
A: Sir.

Q: What do you call a shark with a rocket launcher?
A: Anything he tells you to.

Q: What do you call a neurotic octopus?
A: A crazy, mixed up squid.

Q: What do you call a baby whale that never stops crying?
A: A little blubber.

Q: What kind of sea creature eats its victims two by two?
A: Noah's shark.

Q: What side of a fish has the most scales?
A: The outside.

Q: How do you stick down an envelope under the water?
A: With a seal.

Q: What swims and is highly dangerous?
A: A trout with a hand grenade.

Q: What did one sardine say to the other sardine when it saw a submarine?
A: There goes a can full of people.

Q: What swims in the sea, carries a machine gun and makes you an offer you can't refuse?
A: The Codfather.

Q: What do you give a seasick elephant?
A: Lots of room.

Q: How can you tell when a fisherman is lying?
A: Watch his mouth real close—if it moves he's lying.

Q: Why don't sharks attack lawyers?
A: Professional courtesy.

Q: What do you say to a guy with his lure in the seaweed?
A: Your fly's down!

Q: Why didn't Noah do any fishing on the ark?
A: Because he only had two worms!

Q: Where do you find most of the fish?
A: Between the head and the tail.

Q: How do you stop an old fish from smelling?
A: Peg his nose.

Q: What do you call a couple that go fishing together?
A: Rod and Annette.

Q: If your wife keeps coming out of the kitchen to nag at you about all the time you spend fishing, what have you done wrong?
A: Made her chain too long.

Q: What is the difference between a battery and a woman?
A: A battery has a positive side.

Q: What are the three fastest means of communication?
A: 1. Internet 2. Telephone 3. Tel-a-woman.

Q: What should you give a woman who has everything?
A: A man to show her how to work it.

Q: Why are there no female astronauts on the moon?
A: 'Cause it doesn't need cleaning yet.

FISHERMEN'S BARS

A young fisherman approached a young lady in the bar. He proposed a one dollar bar bet to the well endowed girl that, despite her dress being buttoned to the neck, he could touch her magnificent breasts without touching her clothes.

Since this didn't seem remotely possible, she was intrigued and accepted the bet.

He stepped up, cupped his hands around her breasts and squeezed firmly.

With a baffled look, she said, 'Hey, you touched my clothes!'

And he replied,

'Oh, damn, I owe you a dollar . . .'

An infamous fisherman with a long list of conquests walked into his neighbourhood bar and ordered a drink.

The bartender thought he looked worried and asked him if anything was wrong.

'I'm scared out of my mind,' the stud replied. 'Some pissed-off husband wrote to me and said he'd kill me if I didn't stop sleeping with his wife.'

'So stop,' the barkeep said.

'I can't,' the womaniser replied, taking a long swill. 'The prick didn't sign his name!'

A fishing line and a string walk into a fishermen's bar. The string says to the bartender: 'Hi, a vodka, please.'

The bartender says: 'Sorry, we don't serve strings around here.'

The string leaves and goes around the corner, ties himself in a knot and ruffles his top and bottom.

He goes up to the bartender and again asks for vodka and the bartender says: 'Aren't you the string that just came in here?'

The string replies: 'No, I'm afraid not!'

A pirate with a peg leg, a hook and an eye patch walks into a bar.

The bartender says: 'Where did you get that peg leg?'

The pirate replies: 'We were swimming one day, on the high seas, when a big shark came up and bit off me leg.'

The bartender asks: 'Well, where did you get the hook, then?'

The pirate responded 'We were in a battle with Capt'n Bloodeye and my hand was cut off at the bone.'

The bartender asks: 'Then where did ya get the eye patch?'

The pirate says: One day, I looked up at a gull flying over head and it pooped right in me eye.'

The puzzled bartender says: 'Why would you need an eye patch after that?'

The pirate replies: 'First day with the hook . . .'

A fisherman walks into his club bar and is surprised to find he's the only customer. He asks for a beer, but the barman says 'I'll just be a few minutes sir, I've got to change the barrel—help yourself to the savoury snacks.'

So the man's sitting quietly nibbling the nibbles, when he hears a voice, 'I tell you what, mate, you're looking really good tonight, that suit is really you.'

He looks around, but he's still alone.

Then he hears '. . . and that new haircut, it couldn't be better.'

Again he looks around. Nothing.

'. . . and have you lost weight? I don't think I've ever seen you looking so well.'

Still no-one about.

After a while the barman returns and the man says, 'You won't believe what's happened. I was just sitting here on my own and I heard this voice say I look great, my suit is really me and that I've never looked so well. And yet there's no-one here.'

'Oh,' said the barman, 'that'll be the nuts, they're complimentary.'

A drunk fisherman is in a bar, lying on the floor and looking the worse for wear. Other hotel patrons decide to be good Samaritans and to take him home.

They pick him up off the floor and drag him out the door.

On the way to the car, he falls down three times.

When they get to his house, they help him out of the car and he falls down four more times.

Mission accomplished, they prop him against the door jam and ring the doorbell.

'Here's your husband!' they exclaim proudly.

'Where is his wheelchair?' asked the puzzled wife.

A fisherman walks into a bar carrying a small box. He says to the bartender: 'How much do you think I could make from a dancing fly?'

'A dancing fly?!' says the bartender, 'I thought you just used flies as lures. Let me see it.'

The fisherman opens the box and puts a tiny fly onto the bar, goes over and turns on the jukebox and straight away the fly begins to dance.

'Hey that's pretty good,' says the bartender. 'How long did it take to teach him that?'

'Ten years,' replies the man 'Do you know an agent who could help me make him a star?'

'Sure,' says the bartender. 'See that man over there on the phone? He's in the entertainment game.'

The man puts the fly back in the box, walks over and carefully puts the fly back on the table next to the phone and patiently waits for the man to hang up.

'Yes, of course I will,' says the bloke on the phone. 'No, I won't forget. Okay, thank you, see you.'

Bang, he goes, with the phone on the table.

'Blasted bugs,' he says. 'Now what is it you want?'

Two fat fishermen are sitting in a pub.

One says to the other, 'Your round.'

And the other bloke replies, 'So are you, ya fat bastard!'

A fisherman who was obviously the victim of a nasty accident came staggering into the pub with both arms in plaster casts.

'I'll have a beer, thanks mate,' he said to the barman. 'And could you hold it up to my lips for me?'

'No worries,' said the barman.

'Couldn't light a fag for me, too, could you?' asked the bloke.

'Not a problem,' said the barman.

'Thanks, mate,' said the bloke. 'Me wallet's in me back pocket, if you'd like to get it out for me.'

'There you go,' said the barman.

'Cheers,' said the bloke. 'By the way, where's the toilet?'

And without a moment's hesitation, the barman said, 'Go two blocks up the street, turn right and it's the second on the left.'

FISHING AND CAMPING

Two young men were out in the woods on a camping and fishing trip, when they came upon this great trout brook.

They stayed there all day, enjoying the fishing, which was super.

At the end of the day, knowing that they would be graduating from college soon, they vowed that they would meet, in twenty years, at the same place and renew the experience.

Twenty years later, they met and travelled to a spot near where they had been years before. They walked into the woods and before long came upon a brook.

One of the men said to the other, 'This is the place!'

The other replied, 'No, it's not!'

The first man said, 'Yes, I do recognise the clover growing on the bank on the other side.'

To which the other man replied, 'Silly, you can't tell a brook by its clover.'

Last night I lay in my bed at the camp site, the babbling river running nearby and, looking up at the stars in the sky, I thought to myself, 'Where the hell is the bloody ceiling?'

Bob and Earl were two fishermen who lived for their sport.

They fished at every opportunity and watched all the fishing shows on television. They pored over every magazine article on fishing and discussed tactics on how to win the major fishing competitions.

They even agreed that whoever died first would try to come back and tell the other if there was fishing in heaven.

One summer night, Bob passed away in his sleep after coming in from a big day out fishing. He had had a good day and so he died happy.

A few nights later, his buddy Earl awoke to the sound of Bob's voice from beyond.

'Bob, is that you?' Earl exclaimed. 'This is unbelievable! So tell me, is there fishing in heaven?'

'Well, I have some good news and some bad news for you. Which do you want to hear first?'

'Tell me the good news first.'

'Well, the good news is that, yes, there is fishing in heaven and we go camping and fishing every weekend, Earl.'

'Oh, that is wonderful! So what could possibly be the bad news?'

'You're coming out fishing with me this weekend.'

ON YOUR FISHING TRIP, YOU KNOW THAT YOU HAVE MET A COUNTRY BUMPKIN IF:

- He thinks a stock tip is advice about grooming his hogs.
- 'He needed killing,' is a valid defence.
- He has an 'Elvis' jelly mould.
- His wife owns a home-made fur coat.
- He and his dog use the same tree.
- He vacuums his bed rather than change the sheet.
- Her idea of talking during sex is, 'Ain't no cars coming, baby.'

- His dog and his wallet are both on chains.
- A 'Say No To Crack' sign reminds him to pull up his pants.
- His PC keyboard only goes up to #6.
- His wife keeps a spit cup on the ironing board.
- His diploma says, 'From the Trucking Institute'.
- He thinks Dom Perignon is a Mafia leader.
- He has been too drunk to fish.
- Her idea of a seven course meal is a bucket of KFC and a six pack.
- He says, 'It's so dry, the trees are bribing the dogs.'
- He got his wife's phone number from a wall in a bar's restroom.
- Jack Daniels is on his list of 'Most Admired People'.
- He goes Christmas shopping for her mother, sister and wife and he only needs one gift.
- He borrowed dad's tractor for his first date.
- He can tell his age by the number of rings in her bathtub.
- His beer can collection is considered a tourist attraction in town.
- Going to the bathroom at night requires shoes and a flashlight.
- He gets lost in thought and find himself in unfamiliar territory.
- He thinks Genitalia is an Italian airline.
- He has more buckles than pants.
- One of her kids was born on a pool table.
- He thinks safe sex is a padded headboard.
- His house doesn't have curtains but his truck does.
- He thinks 'loading the dishwasher' means taking his wife out and getting her drunk.
- The coffee table used to be a cable spool.
- The stereo speakers used to belong to the drive in.

- The Halloween pumpkin has more teeth than his wife.
- He thinks dual air bags refers to his wife and his mother-in-law.

TRICKS

SOME JOKES TO PLAY ON YOUR FISHING MATES WHEN YOU ARE CAMPING:

Wait until your victim is asleep.
Smear toothpaste all over your victim's body.
When he wakes up in the morning ask him why he got so crazy with brushing his teeth the night before.

Get all of your victim's items wet, then put them all back in the tent.

When he notices he has nowhere to sleep or has any dry clothes he'll be very mad and very miserable.

Put clear tape on your mate's eyes when he is asleep, wake him up and ask if he feels all right.

This practical joke is an old one that must be done to a person while he or she is sleeping; it was rumoured that it was played by soldiers in barracks during World War 2. A sleeping person's hand is dipped in warm water which apparently causes a subconscious relaxation of the bladder and causes the person to wet his or her bed.

Fasten someone to their bed with numerous bungy cords.

Put coat hangers between the mattress and the sheet.

Get lots of cheap alarm clocks and set them to go off at 3 am and every 20 minutes thereafter. Hide them well.

Pour 'calumet', the stuff in those glow sticks you see every Halloween, on someone then wake them and say, 'Dude, you're glowing' and watch them panic.

Shave parts of a person while they are passed out drunk. Be creative. Do things such as half a moustache, one eyebrow, etc.

Draw in permanent marker all sorts of messages on the skin of a person who has passed out drunk.

Smear a person's body with a hair removal substance. This works great on hairy European guys.

Print a message, such as 'Thank You', in lipstick on someone's chest.

Sprinkle sand in the person's bed.

While a friend is sleeping put shaving cream in both of their hands.

Then tickle his face with a feather or light finger touch.

When making a bed, fold the top sheet in half so that it goes halfway down, then tuck it in like you would if the sheet went all the way to the bottom.

When the victim crawls into bed, they can only get about halfway into bed.

TEST OF CO-ORDINATION

Propose to the victim a co-ordination test and tell him that it has been taken by the brightest people around you (quote some scores!).

Sit in front of the victim and put your palms about twelve inches apart.

The victim's task is very simple.

With eyes closed, his palms clasped together, he should cautiously take his palms between your palms, remove them and repeat the process.

Of course, he must not touch your palms otherwise he 'loses'.

Each cycle counts as one point and 'any average person can get 100 points'.

Tell him the scores of some other people you know.

Let him practise a little with his eyes open.

Then blindfold him (to avoid the natural temptation of cheating) and say 'Start.' After a while leave.

It is a hilarious sight to see a person rock his clasped palms back and forth for no obvious reason.

Be sure to invite many of your friends to witness this sight.

You will find that this co-ordination test really sounds sincere and many innocent people who listen to you explaining to the chosen victim, actually volunteer to take the test before the victim.

This gives you many victims to choose from.

FISHING AND LOVE

A woman is in bed with her lover who also happens to be her husband's best friend. After making love, while they're just laying there, the phone rings.

Since it is the woman's house, she picks up the receiver.

Her lover looks over at her and listens, only hearing her side of the conversation . . .

'Hello? Oh, hi. I'm so glad that you called,' she says speaking in a cheery voice.

'Really? That's wonderful. I am so happy for you, that sounds terrific . . .'

'Great!'

'Thanks.'

'Okay.'

'Bye.'

She hangs up the telephone and her lover asks, 'Who was that?'

'Oh,' she replies, 'that was my husband telling me all about the wonderful time he's having on his fishing trip with you.'

A wife went fishing with her husband.

After several hours, she remarked, 'I haven't had this much fun since the last time that I cleaned the oven.'

WHY BOATS ARE BETTER THAN WOMEN:

- Boats only need their fluids changed every year.

- Boats' curves never sag.
- Boats last longer.
- Boats don't get pregnant.
- You can ride a boat any time of the month.
- Boats don't have parents.
- Boats don't whine unless something is really wrong.
- You can share your boat with your friends.
- If your boat makes too much noise, you can buy a muffler.
- You only need to get a new belt for your boat when the old one is really worn.
- If your boat smokes, you can do something about it.
- Boats don't care about how many other boats you have ridden.
- When riding, you and your boat both arrive at the same time.

- Boats don't care about how many other boats you have.
- Boats don't mind if you look at other boats or if you buy boating magazines.
- If your boat is misaligned, you don't have to discuss politics to correct it.
- You can have a beer while riding your boat.
- You don't have to be jealous of the guy that works on your boat.
- You don't have to deal with priests or blood-tests to register your boat.
- You don't have to convince your boat that you're a boater and that you think that all boats are equals.
- If you say bad things to your boat, you don't have to apologise before you can ride it again.
- You can ride a boat as long as you want and it won't get sore.
- Your parents don't remain in touch with your old boat after you dump it.
- Boats always feel like going for a ride.
- Boats don't insult you if you are a bad boater.
- Boats don't care if you are late.
- You don't have to take a shower before riding your boat.
- It's always okay to use tie downs on your boats.
- If your boat doesn't look good, you can paint it or get better parts.
- You can't get diseases from a boat you don't know very well.

I was given the ultimatum three weeks ago. She said, 'It's me or your fishing.'

Gee I miss her.

I think the only reason my husband likes to go fishing so much is that it's the only time he hears someone tell him, 'Wow, that's a big one!'

A man phones home from his office and tells his wife: 'Something has just come up.'

'I have a chance to go fishing for a week. It's the opportunity of a lifetime and we leave right away. So, be a darling, pack my clothes, my fishing equipment and especially my blue silk pyjamas. I'll be home in an hour to pick them up.'

He goes home in a hurry and grabs everything and rushes off.

A week later he returns.

His wife asks: 'Did you have a good trip, dear?'

He says, 'Oh yes it was great. But you forgot to pack my blue silk pyjamas.'

His wife smiles and says, 'Oh no, I didn't. I put them in your tackle box!'

A couple whose passion had waned saw a marriage counsellor and went through a number of appointments that brought little success. Suddenly at one session the counsellor grabbed the wife and kissed her passionately.

'There,' he said to the husband, 'That's what she needs every Monday, Wednesday, Saturday and Sunday.'

'Well,' replied the husband, 'I can bring her in on Mondays and Wednesdays, but Saturdays and Sundays are my fishing days.'

10 REASONS WHY FISHING MAGAZINES ARE BETTER THAN SEX MAGAZINES

1. You don't have to hide your fishing magazines.
2. If your partner takes pictures or videotapes of you reading fishing magazines, you don't have to worry about them showing up on the Internet if you become famous.
3. Your fishing partner doesn't get upset about you looking at photos of fish that were caught a long time ago.
4. It's perfectly respectable to show your fishing magazine to a total stranger.
5. When you read about a really good fisherperson, you don't have feel guilty about imagining the two of you fishing together.
6. Nobody will ever tell you that you will go blind if you read a fishing magazine by yourself.
7. You don't have to go to a sleazy shop in a seedy neighbourhood to buy a fishing magazine.
8. You can have a calendar from a fishing magazine on your wall at the office without getting sued for harassment.
9. You can read fishing magazines until you are 90 years old and nobody will call you a 'dirty old man'.
10. Your partner will never say, 'No more fishing magazines! You just bought one last week! Is fishing all you ever think about?'

LOVE IS IN THE AIR

WHY FISHING IS BETTER THAN MAKING LOVE:

- When you go fishing and you catch something, that's good. If you're making love and you catch something, that's bad.
- Fish don't compare you to other fishermen. And don't want to know how many other fish you caught.
- In fishing you lie about the one that got away. In loving you lie about the one you caught.
- You can catch and release a fish. You don't have to lie and promise to still be friends after you let it go.
- You don't necessarily have to change your line to keep catching fish.
- You can catch a fish on a 20 cent frozen squid. If you want to catch a woman you're talking dinner and a movie minimum.
- Fish don't mind if you fall asleep in the middle of fishing.

It was cold and wet and windy. Two men met in the street. 'Where're you going?'

'Football.'

'You're mad. In weather like this? Why don't you come with me?'

'Where are you off to?'

'Fishing.'

They walked along the bonnie banks of Loch Lomond. It was a beautiful cloudless day.

A perfect day for love and romance.

'See those birds skimming across the water, flapping their wings a hundred times a minute?' she asked.

'Aye,' he answered softly.

'And do you see they have their beaks together?'

'Aye,' he said.

'Let's do that,' she implored.

'Goodness,' he said breathlessly, 'I'm afraid I can't flap my arms that fast.'

The old couple, still hearty, were celebrating their diamond wedding and to mark the occasion had received a special call from the Parish Minister.

As the visitor was about to leave, he asked if they could name their own special secret to account for their longevity.

'Oh, yes,' answered John readily enough, 'it's marriage!'

The minister beamed with pleasure.

He could hardly wait to hear the further story of domestic harmony over the years.

'Marriage for long life, John,' he replied, 'now that's most interesting.'

But John cut him short.

'You see,' he went on, 'this is the way of it. After I was married I said to the wife, 'Meg,' I says, 'I must warn you that I've a very sharp tongue in my head and I'm thinking that sometimes you'll hear the edge of it. But when you've had as much as you can stand, you can always open the door and go out for a long walk!'

'And Meg said to me, 'Well, John, you'll learn quick enough that I've a very sharp tongue myself! And when things get over hot for you—well, as you say yourself, there's always the open door and a bit of a walk!'

'And so Reverend,' concluded John with a wry smile, 'that's our secret—plenty o' exercise and fresh air.'

'Oh, Sandy,' sighed the wife one morning. 'I'm convinced my mind is almost completely gone!'

Her husband looked up from Fishing Weekly and commented, 'I'm not surprised: You've been giving me a large piece of it every day for going on twenty years.'

After the wedding the young couple drove off on their honeymoon.

Just past the river they stopped and the groom went off through the trees.

After an hour his bride went looking for him.
He was fishing.
'What's going on?' she demanded.
'Are you nagging already?'

FISHING INSPECTORS

This fisherman goes to the river to check an illegal fish trap that he owns.

He looks around to make sure there are no fishing inspectors about and proceeds to pull the fish trap out to check it.

An Inspector steps out of the bushes.

'Aha!' he says; and the fisherman spins around and yells 'Shit!'

The Inspector, who wasn't expecting such a response said, 'Settle down, I'm the fishing inspector.'

'Thank god for that,' said the fisherman, 'I thought you were the bugger who owned this fish trap'.

A fisherman's wife was sitting on the bank of a river when along came the ranger and said, 'Excuse me madam but I need to speak to your husband. Can you tell me where he is?'

Pointing to a clump of reeds, she replied, 'Go over there and look for the pole with a worm on both ends.'

A couple of young guys were fishing at their special pond off the beaten track when out of the bushes jumped the fishing inspector.

Immediately, one of the boys threw his rod down and started running through the woods like a bat out of hell—and hot on his heels came the fishing inspector.

After about a half mile, the guy stopped and stooped over with his hands on his thighs to catch his breath and the fishing inspector finally caught up to him.

'Let's see your fishing licence, boy!' the inspector gasped.

With that, the guy pulled out his wallet and gave the fishing inspector a valid fishing licence.

'Well, son,' said the inspector. 'You must be about as dumb as a box of rocks! You don't have to run from me if you have a valid licence!'

'Yes sir,' replied the young feller. 'But my friend back there, well, he don't have one . . .'

A man, with two buckets of fish, was stopped by a game-warden in a National Park leaving a lake well known for its fishing.

The fishing inspector asked the man, 'Do you have a licence to catch those fish?'

The man replied to the fishing inspector, 'No, sir. These are my pet fish.'

'Pet fish?!' the inspector replied.

'Yes, sir. Every night I take these here fish down to the lake and let them swim around for a while. I whistle and they jump back into their buckets and I take 'em home.'

'That's a bunch of hooey! Fish can't do that!'

The man looked at the fishing inspector for a moment and then said, 'Here, I'll show you. It really works.'

'Okay, I've got to see this!'

The fishing inspector was curious.

The man poured the fish into the river and stood and waited.

After several minutes, the fishing inspector turned to the man and said, 'Well?'

'Well, what?' the man responded.

'When are you going to call them back?' the fishing inspector prompted.

'Call who back?' the man asked.

'The fish!'

'What fish?' the man asked.

The fishing season hasn't opened and a fisherman, who doesn't have a licence, is casting for trout as a stranger approaches and asks, 'Any luck?'

'Any luck? This is a wonderful spot. I took ten out of this stream yesterday,' he boasts.

'Is that so? By the way, do you know who I am?' asks the stranger.

'Nope.'

'Well, meet the new fishing inspector.'

'Oh,' gulped the fisherman. 'Well, do you know who I am?'

'Nope'.

'Meet the biggest liar in the state.'

FISHING IS RELIGION

One day while driving home from his fishing trip in the pouring rain, a man got a flat tyre outside a monastery.

A monk came out and invited him inside to have dinner and spend the night.

The motorist accepted.

That night he had a wonderful dinner of fish and chips.

He decided to compliment the chef.

Entering the kitchen, he asked the cook, 'Are you the fish friar?'

'No,' the man replied, 'I'm the chip monk.'

Three guys were fishing in a lake one day, when Jesus walked across the water and joined them in the boat.

When the three astonished men had settled down enough to speak, the first guy asked humbly, 'Jesus, I've suffered from back pain ever since I took shrapnel in the Vietnam War. Could you help me?'

'Of course, my son,' Jesus said.

And, when he touched the man's back he felt relief for the first time in years.

The second guy, who wore very thick glasses and had a hard time reading and driving, asked if Jesus could do anything about his poor eyesight.

Jesus smiled, removed the man's glasses and tossed them into the lake.

When they hit the water, the man's eyes cleared and he could see everything clearly.

When Jesus turned to the third guy, the guy put his hands out defensively. 'Don't touch me!' he cried. 'I'm on a disability pension.'

One day a nun was fishing and caught a huge, strange-looking fish.

A man was walking by and said, 'Wow! What a nice Gauddam Fish!'

The sister said, 'Sir, you shouldn't use God's name in vain.'

The man replied, 'But that's the species of the fish—a Gauddam Fish.'

The sister nodded and said, 'Oh, okay.'

The nun took the fish back home and said, 'Mother Superior, look at the Gauddam Fish I caught.'

Shocked, the Mother Superior said, 'Sister, you know better than to take the Lord's name like that.'

The nun said, 'I didn't, it is the species of it—a Gauddam Fish.'

So, the Mother Superior said, 'Well, give me the Gauddam Fish and I'll clean it.'

While she was cleaning the fish, Monsignor walked in and the Mother Superior said, 'Monsignor, look at the Gauddam Fish that the sister caught.'

Nearly fainting, Monsignor said, 'Mother Superior, you shouldn't talk like that!'

Mother Superior said, 'But that's the species of it—a Gauddam Fish.'

Monsignor said, 'Well give me the Gauddam Fish and I'll cook it.'

That evening at supper there was a new priest at the table and he said, 'Wow, what a nice fish.'

In reply, the sister said, 'Thank you, I caught the Gauddam Fish.'

And Mother Superior said, 'I cleaned the Gauddam Fish.'

And Monsignor said, 'I cooked the Gauddam Fish.'

The young priest looked around in disbelief, quite shocked and said, 'I like this goddamn place already!'

The Reverend Green encountered one of his parishioners returning from a day's fishing and engaged him in conversation.

'Ah, Lachlan,' he began in his best preaching tone, 'you are a fine fisherman, but I am a fisher of men.'

Lachlan, determined to get home for his dinner cut him short by replying, 'Aye, I was passing your church last Sunday and looked in the window, but you hadn't caught many . . .'

A FISHERMAN'S PRAYER

God grant that I may live to fish
Until my dying day
And when it comes to my last cast
I then most humbly pray
When in the Lord's safe landing net
I'm peacefully asleep
That in his mercy I'll be judged
As big enough to keep.

Three priests were fishing on a boat when they ran out of bait.

The first priest got up and walked across the water to get some more bait.

After two hours they ran out of bait again and the second priest said he would go get more bait, so he got up and walked across the water.

After a few hours of fishing they ran out of bait again and the third priest said he would get more bait.

He stepped out of the boat and went straight to the bottom.

The first priest turned to the second priest and said, 'Do you think we should have told him where the rocks were?'

The harbourmaster was having troubles with his two young boys, so he decided to send them to the Reverend for some help.

The next morning Billy arrived to be put right.

Upon arriving, the Reverend sat him down and sternly asked, 'Where is God?'

Billy sat there speechless, so the Reverend asked louder, 'Where is God?'

Again no answer came from Billy, so the Reverend shook his finger in Billy's face and screamed:

'*Where is God*?'

Billy screamed and bolted from the room, ran right home and dived into his closet, shutting the door behind him.

His older brother Joe watched this, slowly opened the door and asked, 'What happened to you?'

Billy yelled, 'We're in big trouble this time, dude. God is missing and they think *we* did it.'

DIVINE INTERVENTION

A minister, chaplain of the local fisherman's club, had the members and their families gathered in his church for services.

In a loud voice he proclaimed, 'If I had all the beer in the world, I'd pour it in the river.'

With an even louder voice he said, 'If I had all the wine in the world, I'd pour it in the river.'

He then went on and in a booming voice said, 'If I had all the whiskey in the world, I'd pour it in the river.'

At the conclusion of his sermon, the choir leader said, 'For our closing hymn, let us sing hymn number 47, Shall we gather by the river.'

PASSAGE FROM THE DIVINE BOOK OF FISHING

Lo the angler. He riseth in the morning and upsetteth the whole household.

Mighty are his preparations.

He goeth forth with great hope in his heart—and when the day is far spent he returneth, smelling of strong drink and the truth is not in him.

Anonymous.

A country priest loves to fly fish.

It is an obsession of his.

So far this year, the weather has been so bad that he hasn't had a chance to get his beloved waders on and his favourite flies out of their box.

Strangely though, every Sunday the weather has been good, but of course, Sunday is the day he has to go to work.

The weather forecast is good again for the coming Sunday, so he calls a fellow priest, claiming to have lost his voice and to be in bed with the flu.

He asks him to take over his sermon.

The fly fishing priest drives fifty miles to a river near the coast so that no one will recognise him.

An angel up in Heaven keeps watch and sees what the priest was doing.

He tells God who agrees to do something about it.

With the first cast of his line, a huge fish mouth gulps down the fly.

For over an hour the priest runs up and down the river bank, fighting the fish.

At the end, when he finally lands the monster size fish, it turns out to be a world record salmon.

Confused, the angel asks God, 'Why did you let him catch that huge fish? I thought you were going to teach him a lesson.'

God replies, 'I did. Who do you think he's going to tell?'

A pastor, a priest and a rabbi were out for a day of fishing. After getting into the boat they had just pulled away from the dock when the rabbi said, 'Stop the boat I forgot the coffee.'

The pastor who was driving the boat offered to turn around and go back to the dock. The rabbi indicated that there was no need to do this and quickly jumped out of the boat and ran across the water to shore and then to his car to fetch the coffee.

The priest said that he would go too to help with the carrying.

He climbed over the side, skipped across the water behind the rabbi.

They then came back across the water with the picnic things and got back in the boat.

The pastor, not wanting to be shown up by the rabbi and the priest, made an excuse that he needed to go to the toilet and confidently jumped out of the boat attempting to run across the water like the rabbi and the priest.

Instead, he sank quickly to the bottom of the lake.

With that the priest looked at the rabbi, shook his head and remarked that they should have shown him where the rocks were.

'I didn't see you in church last Sunday, Nigel. I hear you were out playing football instead,' said the vicar.

'That's not true, vicar. And I've got the fish to prove it!'

Lord give me the strength to catch a fish
So big, that even I,
When speaking of it to my friends,
May never need to lie.
Anonymous.

FISHING TRIPS

The party had been out fishing in rough water and one man was so ill, he lost his dentures overboard.

When the boat moved into shelter and they started to clean the catch, another member of the party took out his own false teeth and pretended to find them in the stomach of a large snapper he was cleaning.

'Look what I've found,' he said, handing them to the queasy angler. 'Fancy that big snapper swallowing your teeth!'

The seedy one took the teeth, examined them briefly and tossed them overboard.

'Not mine,' he said. 'Some other poor bugger must have lost them.'

Two fishermen got a pilot to fly them from their hometown up to the gulf for a weekend's fishing.

They were quite successful and bagged six huge marlin.

As they started loading the plane for the return trip, the pilot said the plane could only take four of the fish.

The two fishermen strongly objected saying, 'Last year we also caught six and the pilot let us put them all on board and it was also the exact same type of plane, with the exact same capacity.'

Reluctantly, the pilot gave in and all six were loaded.

However, upon take-off the little plane couldn't make it and they crashed in the wilderness.

Climbing out of the wreck one fisherman asked the other, 'Do you know where we are?'

'Yup!' said the second one, 'I think it's pretty close to where we crashed last year.'

One day, on the way home from a fishing trip with his mates, a guy sees a sign in front of a house: 'Talking Dog for Sale'.

He says to his mates, 'I could do with a bit of company while I am out in the boat by myself, I think I will find out about the dog.'

He rings the bell and the owner tells him the dog is in the backyard.

The guy goes into the backyard and sees a black Labrador just sitting there

'You actually talk?' he asks.

'Yep,' the Labrador replies.

'So, what's your story?'

The Labrador looks up and says, 'Well, I discovered this gift pretty young and I wanted to help the government, so I told the CIA about my gift and in no time they had me jetting from country to country, sitting in rooms with spies and world leaders, because no one figured a dog would be eavesdropping.

'I was one of their most valuable spies for eight years running. The jetting around really tired me out and I knew I wasn't getting any younger and I wanted to settle down. So I signed up for a job at the airport to do some undercover security work, mostly wandering near suspicious characters and listening in. I uncovered some incredible dealings there and was awarded a batch of medals. Had a wife, a mess of puppies and now I'm just retired.'

The guy is amazed. He goes back in and asks the owner what he wants for the dog.

'Ten dollars,' he says.

The guy says, 'This dog is amazing. Why on earth are you selling him so cheap?'

'He's a liar. He didn't do any of that stuff.'

Did you hear the one about the lady who went deep-sea fishing with seven fishermen?

She came back with a *big* Red Snapper!

Les and his offsider, Scratch, made a nice thing out of taking tourists out fishing in their boat. One day Les told Scratch about a little problem.

'We've got this party booked for next Wednesday and they're all women. You know we've got no toilet on the boat. How the hell do we explain that to them?'

Scratch wasn't worried at all.

'There's nice ways of saying these things. Like you can use the expression '"evacuate yourself".'

'Well Scratch, how'd it be if you told 'em?'

On the Wednesday morning Les and Scratch were briefing their female charges and Scratch announced, 'There's one other thing, ladies. If you want to evacuate yourselves, you'll have to piss over the side.'

A husband and wife are travelling by car up north where they plan to catch the big ones.

After almost 24 hours on the road, they're too tired to continue and they decide to stop for a rest.

They stop at a nice hotel and take a room, but they only plan to sleep for four hours and then get back on the road as the charter that they have booked is scheduled to leave dock at midday.

When they check out four hours later, the desk clerk hands them a bill for $350.

The man explodes and demands to know why the charge is so high.

He tells the clerk although it's a nice hotel, the rooms certainly aren't worth $350.

When the clerk tells him $350 is the standard rate, the man insists on speaking to the Manager.

The Manager appears, listens to the man and then explains that the hotel has an Olympic-sized pool and a huge conference centre that were available for the husband and wife to use.

'But we didn't use them,' the man complains.

'Well, they are here and you could have,' explains the Manager.

He goes on to explain they could have taken in one of the shows for which the hotel is famous.

'The best entertainers from New York, Hollywood and Las Vegas perform here,' the Manager says.

'But we didn't go to any of those shows,' complains the man again.

'Well, we have them and you could have,' the Manager replies.

No matter what facility the Manager mentions, the man replies, 'But we didn't use it!'

The Manager is unmoved and eventually the man gives up and agrees to pay.

He writes a cheque and gives it to the Manager.

The Manager is surprised when he looks at the cheque. 'But sir,' he says, 'this cheque is only made out for $50.'

'That's right,' says the man. 'I charged you $300 for sleeping with my wife.'

'But I didn't!' exclaims the Manager.

'Well,' the man replies, 'she was here and you could have.'

There was a crowd of more than five thousand bearded characters in long robes standing on the bank of the Sea of Galilee.

They had been there for hours and it was lunch time.

The only food that came to light was five barley loaves and three fishes.

Philip said to James, 'Look at that. Another typical logistics cock-up.'

GUIDE TO COUNTRY MEDICAL TERMS FOR FISHERMEN ON A WEEKEND AWAY:

Bacteria	Back door to cafeteria.
Benign	What you be after you be eight.

Barium	What you do with dead folks.
Caesarean section	A neighbourhood in Rome.
CAT scan	Searching for the cat.
Cauterise	Made eye contact with her.
Colic	A sheep dog.
Coma	A punctuation mark.
D & C	Where Washington is.
Dilate	To live longer than your kids do.
Enema	Not a friend.
Fester	Quicker than someone else.
Fibula	A small lie.
GI Series	World Series of military baseball.
Hangnail	What you hang your coat on.
Hospital	The biggest building in town.
Impotent	Distinguished, well known.
Labour Pain	Getting hurt at work.
Medical Staff	A doctor's walking stick.
Morbid	A higher offer than I bid.
Nitrates	Cheaper than day rates.
Node	I knew it.
Outpatient	A person who has fainted.
Pap Smear	A fatherhood test.
Pelvis	Second cousin to Elvis.
Post Operative	A letter carrier.
Recovery Room	Place to do upholstery.
Secretion	Hiding something.
Tablet	A small table to change babies on.
Seizure	Roman emperor who lived in the Caesarean section.
Terminal Illness	Getting sick at the train station.
Tumour	More than one.
Urine	Opposite of mine.
Varicose	Near by.

Two men were preparing to go out for a day's fishing on the bay.

While one of them got the boat ready, the other went to his friend's house to pick up some gear that had been left on the veranda.

While he was there, he saw a man in bed with his friend's wife.

Back at the boat he announced that he had some bad news and said what he had seen. His friend took it calmly:

'Is that all? I was afraid you were going to say the bass weren't biting.'

OUT IN THE STICKS

The manager of the Riverside Caravan Park always greeted the fishermen at the end of the day by asking, 'How did you do?'

Late one afternoon he saw a man's head appear and asked his usual question, 'How did you do?'

The response was quite angry.

Then he saw that the man was carrying a rug and cushion and had a pretty girl by his side. He wasn't even carrying a hand line.

A woman walking along a beach came upon a man fast asleep with a fishing rod gripped in his hand. The line was jerking so she woke him up.

'Wake up mister. You've got a bite.'

'Oh, would you mind reeling it in for me please?'

She did this and landed his fish for him.

'Could you put some fresh bait on the hook and cast it out for me, please?'

She grinned and baited his hook.

'A man as lazy as you should be married and have a son to help him.'

'That's an idea. I wonder where I can find a pregnant girl.'

An angler was going off for a weekend's fishing. His wife said to him: 'Just in case you don't catch any fish to eat, take along this packet of sausages.'

'How do you cook them?'

'It's easy. The same as you do your fish.'

The weekend was not a success. The fisherman didn't get a touch. He was bad tempered and hungry when he got home.

'Those sausages you gave me wouldn't feed the cat. By the time I skinned them and gutted them and cleaned them there wasn't enough left to make a decent feed.'

Bobby was in the fishing tackle department. 'Do you have any left-handed fish hooks please? I'm left-handed.'

'We'll go through them and see.'

The assistant brought out every box of hooks that he had and examined each one closely.

By the time he finished the counter was covered with fish hooks.

'I'm afraid you're out of luck, sir,' said the assistant at last.

'There don't seem to be any left-handed fish hooks in stock at all.'

'Never mind,' said Bobby. 'Give us a couple of dozen of those. I'll just have to fish from the left-hand side of the boat.'

A passer-by came upon a man fishing in a pool of rainwater.

'What do you think you might get?'

'Trout.'

'What? There are no trout there. In fact there are no fish at all.'

'Well, if there are no fish at all, I might as well fish for trout as anything else.'

'Anyway, the season's closed for trout.'

'Is it? I'm glad you told me. I'll put a bigger hook on and fish for bream.'

It was late at night and father was out fishing and mother, who was expecting her second child, was home alone with her three-year old daughter.

The woman started going into labour and so she called 000.

Due to a power outage at the time, only one paramedic responded to the call.

The house was very, very dark, so the paramedic asked the three year old to hold a flashlight high over her mother so he could see while he helped deliver the baby.

Very diligently, the child did as she was asked.

The mother laboured and pushed and pushed and, after a little while a new baby boy was born.

The paramedic lifted him by his little feet and spanked

him on his bottom. Connor began to cry.

The paramedic then thanked the child for her help and asked the wide-eyed three-year old what she thought about what she had just witnessed.

She quickly responded:

'He shouldn't have crawled in there in the first place. Smack him again!'

A woman takes a lover home while her husband is out fishing.

Her nine-year-old son comes home unexpectedly, sees them and hides in the bedroom closet to watch.

The woman's husband also comes home.

She puts her lover in the closet, not realising that the little boy is in there already.

The little boy says, 'Dark in here.'

The man says, 'Yes, it is.'

Boy: 'I have a baseball.'

Man: 'That's nice.'

Boy: 'Want to buy it?'

Man: 'No, thanks.'

Boy: 'My dad's outside.'

Man: 'Okay, how much?'

Boy: '$250.'

In the next few weeks, it happens again that the boy and the lover are in the closet together.

Boy: 'Dark in here.'

Man: 'Yes, it is.'

Boy: 'I have a baseball glove.'

The lover remembering the last time, asks the boy, 'How much?'

Boy: '$750.'

Man: 'Fine.'

A few days later, the father says to the boy, 'Grab your glove, let's go outside and have a game of catch.'

The boy says, 'I can't, I sold my baseball and my glove.'

The father asks, 'How much did you sell them for?'

Boy: '$1000.'

The father says, 'That's terrible to overcharge your friends like that, that is way more than those two things cost. I'm going to take you to church and make you confess.'

They go to the church and the father makes the boy sit in the confession booth and he closes the door.

The boy says, 'Dark in here.'

The priest says, 'Don't start that again.'

FISHING WIDOWS

A fisherman's wife gave birth to twin boys.

When the babies were side by side, they always looked in opposite directions, so they were named Forward and Away.

Years later the fisherman took his sons fishing, but they didn't return.

Months passed and the wife finally spotted her husband plodding sadly up the beach. He explained to her that during their trip, Forward had hooked an enormous fish.

He had struggled for hours, when suddenly the fish pulled Forward into the water and they never saw him again.

'That's just terrible!' his wife said.

'It was terrible all right,' said the fisherman.

'But you should have seen the one that got Away.'

Q: How much fishing tackle can a man accumulate before his wife throws him out?

A: I don't know the answer, but I think I'm nearly there.

Mother's advice to daughter:

Cook a man a fish and you feed him for a day.

But teach a man to fish and you get rid of him for the whole weekend.

Wanted: Woman who can cook, clean, wash and make sweet love.

Must have own boat.

If interested, send a photo of the boat to . . .

Standing at the edge of the lake, a man saw a woman flailing about in the deep water.

Unable to swim, the man screamed for help.

A trout fisherman ran up.

The man said, 'My wife is drowning and I can't swim. Please save her. I'll give you a hundred dollars.'

The fisherman dived into the water.

In ten powerful strokes, he reached the woman, put his arm around her and swam back to shore.

Depositing her at the feet of the man, the fisherman said,

'Okay, where's my hundred dollars?'

The man said, 'Look, when I saw her going down for the third time, I thought it was my wife. But this is my mother-in-law.'

The fisherman reached into his pocket and said, 'Just my luck. How much do I owe you?'

Billy Bob happened to mention that his wife was an angel and Bubba said, 'You're lucky. Mine's still alive.'

Q: How can a fisherman tell if his wife is dead?
A: The sex is the same, but the dishes pile up.

Mrs Pete Johnson came into the newsroom to pay for her husband's obituary.

She was told by the kindly newsman that it was a dollar a word and he remembered Pete and how he loved his fishing and wasn't it too bad about him passing away.

She thanked him for his kind words and bemoaned the fact that she only had two dollars.

But she wrote out the obituary, 'Pete died.'

The newsman said he thought old Pete deserved more and he'd give her three more words at no charge.

Mrs Pete Johnson thanked him and rewrote the obituary: 'Pete died. Boat for sale.'

HUNTING AND FISHING

In the middle of the forest, a hunter is confronted by a mean and angry grizzly bear.

He takes his gun and takes aim, but fear overcomes him and he cannot shoot.

So he turns to run for his life.

He runs and runs.

His lungs are burning and he cannot get his breath.

He feels that his heart is about to burst from his chest.

He finds himself at the edge of a very steep cliff.

He can't go over it; he can't go through it; he can't go under it.

He is trapped.

So he does what any reasonable person might do in these situations.

He kneels down and prays to God.

'Dear Lord, Spare me. Please give this bear some religion,' he implores.

The thunder rumbles, the skies darken and a streak of lightning shoots through the air.

The bear stops abruptly, looks around and looks to the sky.

'For what I am about to receive, I give thanks Oh lord. I thank thee for the food I am about to eat.'

Two blonde duck-shooters were out shooting ducks.

One took aim and hit a bird which tumbled out of the sky to land at his feet.

'Ah, you should have saved the bullet,' said the other. 'The fall would have killed him, anyway.'

A young man is on his honeymoon near his favourite fishing spot.

He hires a fishing guide and spends his days fishing.

The guide mentions to him that, for a man on his honeymoon, he is spending an awful lot of time fishing.

The young man replies, 'Oh, you know how I love to fish.'

'But aren't you newlyweds supposed to spend your days and nights making love?' asked the guide.

'Yes, that's right, but she has gonorrhoea and you just know how I love to fish.'

The guide said that he understood but that there were other ways to have sex.

'I know, but she has diarrhoea and you know how I love to fish.'

The guide says he understands but there are other ways that they might have sex.

'Yes, but she has pyuria and you know how I love to fish.'

'Why on earth would you marry somebody with health problems like that?'

'It's because she has worms and you know how I love to fish.'

Two hunters are out looking for ducks when they come across a local farmer's daughter, sitting naked on a hillock, sunning herself.

'Are you game?' the first hunter asks.

'Yes, I am,' replies the maiden.

So the second hunter shoots her.

A man and his grandson are having a bonding session out by the lake fishing together. Grandad takes out a cigarette, lights it and draws back hungrily.

'Grandad, can I have one of those cigarettes?' asked the wee tacker.

'Can you touch your arsehole with your penis?' asked grandad.

'No.'

'Then you are not old enough.'

Grandad takes out a beer and takes the top off. He takes a long sip and breaths a happy sigh.

'Grandad, can I have a beer then?' asked the little fellow.

'Can you touch your arsehole with your penis?'

'No.'

'Then you are not old enough.'

They continue to fish and after a time the young man gets hungry and reaches into his back pack to take out some of the cookies his mother had made for him to take with him.

He takes a bite and munches away happily.

'They look good,' said Grandpa, 'Can I please have one?'

'Can you touch your arsehole with your penis, Grandad?'

'I most certainly can.'

'Then go screw yourself. These are my cookies.'

There's a Kiwi rugby fan, an Australian rugby fan and a gorgeous woman sitting next to each other on a train. The train goes through a tunnel and everything gets dark. Suddenly there's a kissing sound and then a 'SLAP!'

The train comes out of the tunnel and the woman and the Australian are sitting there looking perplexed.

The Kiwi is bent over holding his face which is red from an apparent slap. He's thinking, 'That Australian must have tried to kiss this lady, she thought it was me and slapped me.'

The lady is thinking, 'That Kiwi must have gone to kiss me, kissed the Australian instead and got slapped.'

The Australian is thinking to himself, 'If this train goes through another tunnel, I could make another kissing sound and smack that Kiwi in the head again.'

ROOTIN', SHOOTIN' AND TOOTIN'

An 80 year old man was having his annual check-up and the doctor asked him how he was feeling. 'I've never been better!' he boasted. 'I've got an eighteen year old bride who's pregnant and having my child! What do you think about that?'

The doctor considered this for a moment, then said, 'Let me tell you a story. I knew a guy who was an avid hunter. He never missed a season. But one day he went out in a bit of a hurry and accidentally grabbed his umbrella instead of his gun.'

The doctor continued, 'So he was in the woods and suddenly a grizzly bear appeared in front of him! He raised up his umbrella, pointed it at the bear and squeezed the handle. And do you know what happened?' the doctor queried.

Dumbfounded, the old man replied, 'No.'

The doctor continued, 'The bear dropped dead in front of him!'

'That's impossible!' exclaimed the old man. 'Someone else must have shot that bear.'

'That's kind of what I'm getting at . . .' replied the doctor.

A young man has just come home from a day's fishing and is in bed with his wife watching 'Who Wants to be a Millionaire.'

The husband asks for sex.
The wife says, 'No.'
Her husband asks, 'Is that your final answer?'
She responds, 'Yes.'
He says, 'Then, I'd like to phone a friend.'

An old fisherman goes to the Wizard to ask him if he can remove a curse he has been living with for the last 40 years.

The Wizard says, 'Maybe, but you will have to tell me the exact words that were used to put the curse on you.'

The old man says without hesitation, 'I now pronounce you man and wife.'

On hearing that her elderly grandfather had just passed away, Jenny went straight over to visit her grandmother.

'Grandma, it's so sad, I loved grandpa. He used to take

me fishin' and everything. I'm going to miss him. How did he die?'

Her grandmother explained, 'He had a heart attack during sex on Sunday morning.'

Horrified, Jenny suggested that shagging at the age of 94 was surely asking for trouble.

'Oh no,' her granny replied, 'we had sex every Sunday morning, in time with the church bells—in with the dings and out with the dongs.'

She then paused and wiped away a tear. 'If the ice cream truck hadn't gone by, he'd still be alive today.'

A fisherman who is visiting a small town with his mates, sees a circus banner reading, 'Don't Miss the Amazing Naval Aviator'.

Curious, he buys a ticket.

The tent goes dark.

Suddenly, trumpets blare and all eyes turn to the centre ring.

There, spot lit in the centre ring is a table with three walnuts on it.

Standing next to it is an old retired Naval Aviator.

Suddenly the old man unzips his pants, whips out a huge shlong and smashes all three walnuts with three mighty swings!

The crowd erupts in applause as the elderly Naval Aviator is carried off on the shoulders of the clowns.

Ten years later the fisherman visits the same little town and he sees a faded sign for the same circus and the same 'Don't Miss the Amazing Naval Aviator.'

He can't believe the old guy is still alive much less still doing his act!

So he buys a ticket.

Again, the centre ring is illuminated.

This time, instead of walnuts, three coconuts are on the table.

The Naval Aviator stands before them, then suddenly unzips his fly and smashes the coconuts with three swings of his amazing shlong.

The crowd goes wild!

Flabbergasted, the salesman requests a meeting with him after the show.

'You're incredible,' he tells the Naval Aviator.

'But I have to know something. You're older now. Why switch from walnuts to coconuts?'

'Well,' says the Naval Aviator, 'My eyes aren't what they used to be.'

A man sat at a bar, with the saddest hangdog expression.

Bartender: 'What's the matter? Are you having troubles with your wife?'

The man: 'We had a fight and she told me that she wasn't going to speak to me for a month.'

Bartender: 'That should make you happy.'

The man: 'No, the month is up today!'

RUMINATIONS

THINGS TO PONDER ON A SLOW DAY'S FISHING:

- Jesus loves you . . . but everyone else thinks you are a knob.
- Everyone has a photographic memory, some just don't have any film.
- I used to have a handle on life . . . but it broke off.
- Guys—just because you have one, doesn't mean you have to be one . . .
- Some people just don't know how to drive . . . I call these people 'Everybody But Me'.
- Heart Attacks . . . God's revenge for eating his animal friends.
- Don't like my driving? Then quit watching me.
- 'I can't go to work today, the voices said stay home and clean the boat.'
- Some people are only alive because it is illegal to shoot them.
- Try not to let your mind wander . . . It is too small and fragile to be out by itself.
- Hang up and drive!
- The eyes are the second thing to go. I forget the first . . .
- I planted some bird seed. A bird came up. Now I don't know what to feed it.
- I had amnesia once . . . or twice.
- I went to San Francisco. I found someone's heart.
- Last week I forgot how to ride a bicycle.
- Photons have mass? I didn't even know they were Catholic.

- All I ask is a chance to prove that money can't make me happy.
- I'd give my right arm to be ambidextrous.
- A beggar asked me for 50 cents for a sandwich. I said, 'First let me see the sandwich.'
- What is a 'free' gift? Aren't all gifts free?
- They told me I was gullible . . . and I believed them.
- Teach a child to be polite and courteous in the home and, when he grows up, he'll never be able to edge his car onto a freeway.
- Two can live as cheaply as one, for half as long.
- If God didn't want us to eat animals, why did he make them out of meat?
- Experience is the thing you have left when everything else is gone.
- What if there were no hypothetical questions?

- One nice thing about egotists: they don't talk about other people.
- When the only tool you own is a hammer, every problem begins to look like a nail.
- What was the greatest thing before sliced bread?
- My weight is perfect for my height—which varies.
- I used to be indecisive. Now, I'm not sure.
- The cost of living hasn't affected its popularity.
- How can there be self-help 'groups'?
- Is there another word for synonym?
- Where do forest rangers go to 'get away from it all'?
- The speed of time is one second per second.
- Is it possible to be totally partial?
- What's another word for thesaurus?
- If you're cross-eyed and have dyslexia, can you read all right?
- Is Marx's tomb a communist plot?
- If swimming is so good for your figure, how do you explain whales?
- Show me a man with both feet firmly on the ground and I'll show you a man who can't get his pants off.
- It's not an optical illusion. It just looks like one.
- As three-quarters of the earth's surface is water and only one quarter is land, it seems logical that man should spend three-quarters of his time fishing and one-quarter at work.
- If a fishing inspector and an insurance agent were both drowning and you could only save one of them, would you go to lunch or would you continue reading your paper?

READY TO GO!

A man wakes up at the crack of dawn to go duck hunting. He gets to his blind just before sunrise and settles in.

Over the trees comes a perfect wedge.

BOOM!

He takes out the lead duck and watches as it falls from the sky, bounces off of a barn, hits the fence and lands in the yard of the nearby farm.

The hunter sees no activity at the farm house and decides no one will even notice if he quickly retrieves his trophy.

Just as he lays his hand on the duck he hears a shotgun rack a round in the chamber.

He looks up to hear the farmer ask, 'What ye' doing here?'

The hunter replies, 'Getting my duck there.'

'Reckon that's my duck, hit my barn, my fence and that makes it my duck,' said the farmer.

The hunter was not one to quit and attempts to argue.

This gets him nowhere.

'I reckon there's only one way to settle this, boy and that's the country way. I kick you in the groin, you kick me in the groin and whoever is left standing gets the duck.'

The hunter has no choice but to agree.

The farmer then says, 'I'm going first.'

The farmer leaps off the porch at a dead sprint and kicks the hunter with all he's worth right in the jewels.

The hunter spasms to the ground gasping for air.

It takes him 30 minutes to regain composure and attempt to stand.

Hobbling, the hunter says, 'It's my turn now.'

But the farmer replies, 'Keep your old duck, I don't want it any more.'

The Americans and Russians at the height of the arms race realised that if they continued in the usual manner they were going to blow up the whole world. One day they sat down and decided to settle the whole dispute with one dog fight. They would have five years to breed the best fighting dog in the world and whoever's dog won would be the country entitled to dominate the world.

The Russians found the biggest, meanest Doberman and Rottweiler female dogs in the world and bred them with the biggest, meanest Siberian wolves. They selected only the biggest and strongest puppy from each litter and removed his siblings, which gave him all the milk. After five years they came up with the biggest, meanest dog the world had ever seen.

Its cage needed steel bars that were five inches thick and nobody could get near it.

When the day came for the dog fight, the Americans showed up with a strange animal. It was a nine foot long Dachshund. Everyone felt sorry for the Americans because they knew there was no way that this dog could possibly last ten seconds with the Russian dog.

When the cages were opened up, the Dachshund came out of its cage and slowly waddled over towards the Russian dog. The Russian dog snarled and leaped out of its cage and charged the American dachshund. But, when it got close enough to bite the Dachshund's neck, the

Dachshund opened its mouth and consumed the Russian dog in one bite.

There was nothing left at all of the Russian dog.

The Russians came up to the Americans shaking their heads in disbelief. 'We don't understand how this could have happened. We had our best people working for five years with the meanest Doberman and Rottweiler female dogs in the world and the biggest meanest Siberian wolves.'

'That's nothing,' an American replied. 'We had our best plastic surgeons working for five years to make an alligator look like a Dachshund.'

A fresh faced lad and his father are out fishing on the eve of the son's wedding.

'Dad, why are wedding dresses white?'

The father looks at his son and replies, 'Son, all domestic appliances are white.'

One night, at the lodge of a hunting club, two new members were being introduced to other members and shown around.

The man leading them around said, 'See that old man asleep in the chair by the fireplace? He is our oldest member and can tell you some hunting stories you'll never forget.'

They woke up the old man and asked him to tell them a hunting story.

'Well, I remember back in 1944, we went on a lion hunting expedition in Africa,' he said.

'We were on foot and hunted for three days without

seeing a thing. On the fourth day, I was so tired I had to rest my feet. I found a fallen tree, so I laid my gun down, propped my head on the tree and fell asleep. I don't know how long I was asleep when I was awakened by a noise in the bushes. I was reaching for my gun when the biggest lion I ever seen jumped out of the bushes at me like this and I heard . . . ROAR! . . . I tell you, I just shit my pants.'

The young men looked astonished and one of them said, 'I don't blame you, I would have shit my pants too if a lion jumped out at me.'

The old man shook his head and said, 'No, no, not then, just now when I said ROAR!'

A shy young fisherman goes into The Happy Catch bar and sees a beautiful woman sitting at the bar. After an hour of gathering up his courage he finally goes over to her and asks, tentatively, 'Um, would you mind if I chatted with you for a while?'

She responds by yelling, at the top of her lungs, 'No, I won't sleep with you tonight!' Everyone in the bar is now staring at them.

Naturally, the guy is hopelessly and completely embarrassed and he slinks back to his table.

After a few minutes, the woman walks over to him and apologises. She smiles at him and says, 'I'm sorry if I embarrassed you. You see, I'm a graduate student in psychology and I'm studying how people respond to embarrassing situations.'

To which he responds, at the top of his lungs, 'What do you mean $200?'

'What's the usual tip?' a man growled when, Jason, a uni student, delivered his pizza.

'Well,' Jason replied, 'this is my first delivery, but the other guys said that if I got a quarter out of you, I'd be doing great.'

'Is that so?' grunted the grizzled old fisherman. 'In that case, here's five dollars.'

'Thanks,' Jason said, 'I'll put it in my savings account.'

'By the way, what are you studying?' questioned the man.

Jason replied, 'Applied Psychology.'

One day mum was cleaning Junior's room and in the closet she found an S & M magazine. This was very upsetting for her.

She hid the magazine until his father got home from a fishing weekend with the boys and showed it to him. He looked at it and handed it back to her without a word.

She finally asked him, 'Well, what should we do about this?'

Dad looked at her and said, 'Well, I don't think you should spank him.'

One day this guy, who has been stranded on a desert island all alone for ten years, sees an unusual speck on the horizon. 'It's certainly not a ship,' he thinks to himself.

And as the speck gets closer and closer, he begins to rule out the possibilities of a small boat, then even a raft.

Suddenly, emerging from the surf comes this drop-dead gorgeous blonde woman wearing a wet suit and scuba gear.

She approaches the stunned guy and asks, 'How long has it been since you've had a cigarette?'

'Ten years!' he says.

She reaches over and unzips a waterproof pocket on her left sleeve and pulls out a pocket of fresh cigarettes. He takes one, lights it and takes a long drag and says, 'Man, oh man! Is that ever good!'

She then asks him, 'How long has it been since you've had a sip of bourbon?'

Trembling, he replies, 'Ten years!'

She reaches over, unzips her waterproof pocket on her right sleeve, pulls out a flask and gives it to him. He opens the flask, takes a long swing and says, 'Wow, that's absolutely fantastic!'

Then she starts slowly unzipping the long zipper that runs down the front of her wet suit, looks at him seductively and asks, 'And how long has it been since you've played around?'

The guy, with tears in his eyes, replies, 'Oh sweet Lord God! Don't tell me you've got a computer with internet access in there!'

HEINOUS ENVY . . .

WHEN YOU'RE OUT ON THE BOAT AND HAVEN'T GOT ANYTHING TO TALK ABOUT:

My dick is so big, it graduated a year ahead of me from high school.

My dick is so big, I have to call it Mr Dick in front of company.

My dick is so big, it has an agent.

My dick is so big, it won't return Spielberg's calls.

My dick is so big, it was overthrown by a military coup. It's now known as the Democratic Republic of My Dick.

My dick is so big, it has casters.

My dick is so big, it lives next door.

My dick is so big, it votes.

My dick is so big, the tip started to celebrate the dawn of the millennium, 45 minutes before my balls did.

No matter where I go, my dick always gets there first.

My dick takes longer lunches than I do . . .

My dick is so big, it has feet.

My dick is so big, it has investors.

My dick is so big, we use it at parties as a limbo pole.

My dick is so big, it has an opening act.

My dick is so big, every time I get hard, I cause a solar eclipse.

If you cut my dick in two, you can tell how old I am.

My dick is so big, Trump owns it.

My dick is so big, I can never sit in the front row.

My dick is so big, it has its own dick. And even my dick's dick is bigger than your dick.

My dick is so big, it only does one show a night.

My dick is so big, you can ski down it.

My dick is so big, it has elbows.

My dick is so big, I have to check it as luggage when I fly.

My dick is so big, it has a personal trainer.

My dick is so big, it has a retractable dome.

My dick is so big, it has its own gravity.

My dick is so big, it has a spine.

My dick is so big, it has a basement.

My dick is more muscular than I am.

My dick is so big it has cable.

My dick is so big, it violates seventeen zoning laws.

My dick is so big, I can braid it.

My dick is so big, that when it's Eastern Standard Time at the tip, it's Central Time at my balls.

My dick is so big, I painted the foreskin red, white and blue and used it as a flag.

My dick is so big, I can sit on it.

My dick is so big, it can chew gum.

My dick is so big, it only tips with hundreds.

My dick is so big, Michael Jackson wants to build an amusement park on it.

My dick is so big, you're standing on it.

My dick is so big, it only comes into work when it feels like it.

My dick is so big, it plays golf with the prime minister.

My dick is so big, it charges money for its autograph.

TOP SALES

A keen country lad applied for a salesman's job at a city department store. It was one of those massive stores that has every department imaginable. In fact it was the biggest store in the world—you could get anything there.

The boss asked him, 'Have you ever been a salesman before?'

'Yes, I was a salesman in the country,' said the lad.

The boss liked the cut of him and said, 'You can start tomorrow, Friday morning and I'll come and see you when we close up.'

When the boss looked up the young man the next day at closing time, he saw him shaking hands with a beaming customer. After they parted, he walked over and asked, 'Well, that looked good! How many sales did you make today?'

'That was the only one,' said the young salesman.

'Only one?!' blurted the boss. 'Most of my staff make 20 or 30 sales a day. You'll have to do better than that! Well, how much was the sale worth?'

'$227,334 and change,' said the young man.

The boss paused for a moment, blinking a few times. 'H . . . H . . . How did you manage that?!'

'Well, when he came in this morning I sold him a small fish hook. Then, I sold him a medium hook and then a really large hook. Then I sold him a small fishing line, a medium one and then a big one. I then sold him a spear gun, a wetsuit, scuba gear, nets, chum, coolers and a keg of beer. I asked him where he was going fishing and he said down the coast. We decided he would probably need a new boat, so I took him down to the boat department and sold him that twenty-foot schooner with the twin engines. Then, he said that his Volkswagen probably wouldn't be able to pull it, so I took him to the car department and sold him the new Deluxe Cruiser, with a winch, storage rack, rust proofing and a built-in refrigerator. Oh and floor mats.'

The boss took two steps back and asked in astonishment, 'You sold all that to a guy who came in for a fish hook?!'

'No,' answered the salesman. 'He came in to buy a blanket.'

'A blanket?'

'Yeah, an extra blanket for the couch. He just had a fight with his wife. I said to him, 'Well, your weekend's ruined, so you may as well go fishing . . .'

A married couple is driving down the freeway doing 80 km/h. The husband is behind the wheel. His wife looks over at him and says, 'Honey, I know we've been married for 15 years, but I want a divorce.'

The husband says nothing but slowly increases speed to 90 km/h.

She says, 'I don't want you to try to talk me out of it, because while you've been off fishing so much, I've been having an affair with your best friend and he's a better lover than you.'

Again the husband stays quiet and just speeds up as his anger increases.

She says, 'I want the house.'

Again the husband speeds up and now is doing 100 km/h.

She says, 'I want the kids too.'

The husband just keeps driving faster and faster, now he's up to 120 km/h.

She says, 'I want the car, the checking account and all the credit cards too.'

The husband slowly starts to veer towards the bridge overpass piling, as she says, 'Is there anything you wanted?'

The husband says, 'No, I've got everything I need.'

She asks, 'What's that?'

The husband replies just before they hit the wall at 160 km/h, 'I've got the airbag!'

I'LL DRINK TO THAT!

A bloke goes into a bar with his dog and asks for a drink. The bartender says, 'You can't bring that dog in here!'

The bloke, without missing a beat, says, 'This is my seeing-eye dog.'

'Oh man, I'm sorry,' the bartender says, 'I didn't realise you were blind. Here, the first drink's on me.'

The man takes his drink and goes to a table near the door.

Another guy, a fisherman who has just come in from a day's fishing with his little dog and doesn't want to leave him outside lest he gets too cold, walks into the bar with a Chihuahua.

The first bloke sees him, stops him and says: 'They don't allow dogs in here, so you won't get a drink unless you tell him it's a seeing-eye dog.'

The second man graciously thanks the first man and continues to the bar.

He asks for a drink. The bartender says, 'Sorry, you can't bring that dog in here!'

The second man replies, 'But this is my seeing-eye dog.'

The bartender peers over the edge and says: 'No, I don't think so. They do not have Chihuahuas as seeing-eye dogs.'

The man pauses for a half-second and replies 'What?! They gave me a Chihuahua?'

'Hey, buddy, what's a 'breathalyser?' asked a drunk fisherman of his barman.

'That's a bag that tells you when you've drunk too much,' answered the barman.

'Ah hell, whaddya know? I've been married to one of those for years.'

A group of loud and rowdy fishermen was making a hell of a racket in the street after a big night celebrating the massive catch that George had made.

It was in the wee small hours of the morning and the lady of the house flung open a window and shouted at them to keep quiet.

'Is this where George lives?' one of the drunks asked.

'Yes, it is,' the woman replied.

'Well then,' said the drunk, 'could you come and pick him up so the rest of us can go home?'

Every night, Frank who worked hard on the boats all day, would go down to the liquor store, get a six-pack, bring it home and drink it while he watched TV.

One night, as he finished his last beer, the doorbell rang.

He stumbled to the door and found a six-foot cockroach standing there.

The bug grabbed him by the collar and threw him across the room, then left.

The next night, after he finished his fourth beer, the doorbell rang.

He walked slowly to the door and found the same huge cockroach standing there.

The big bug punched him in the stomach, then left.

The next night, after Frank finished his first beer, the doorbell rang again.

The same six-foot cockroach was standing there.

This time Frank was kneed in the groin and hit behind the ear as he doubled over in pain. Then the big bug left.

The fourth night Frank didn't drink at all.

The doorbell rang.

The cockroach was standing there.

The bug beat the snot out of Frank and left him in a heap on the living room floor.

The following day, Frank went to see his doctor.

He explained the events of the preceding four nights. 'I thought it might be the drink. But he belted me when I didn't have a beer. What can I do?' Frank pleaded.

'Not much,' the doctor replied. 'There's just a nasty bug going around.'

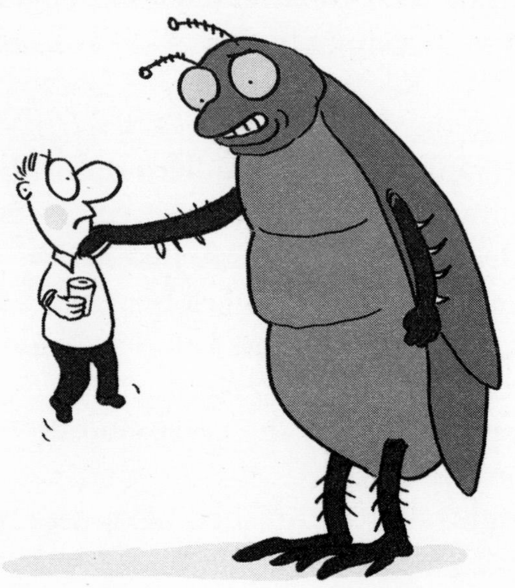

A woman and a man are involved in a bad car accident with a fisherman who was on his way home from weekend sport.

Both cars are written off, but thankfully neither are hurt.

After they crawl out of their cars, the woman says, 'So you're a man; that's interesting. I'm a woman. Gee, just look at our cars! There's nothing left, but fortunately we are unhurt. This must be a sign from God that we should meet and be friends and live together for the rest of our days.'

Flattered, the man replied, 'Oh yes, I agree with you completely! This must be a sign from God!'

The woman continued, 'And look at this, here's another miracle. My car is completely demolished but this bottle of wine didn't break. Surely God wants us to drink this wine and celebrate our good fortune.'

Then she hands the bottle to the man. The man nods his head in agreement, opens it and drinks half the bottle and then hands it back to the woman. The woman takes the bottle, immediately puts the cap back on and hands it back to the man.

The man asks, 'Aren't you having any?'

The woman replies, 'No. I think I'll just wait for the police.'

Scientists for Health Canada suggest that drinking beer makes men act like women.

To test the theory, 100 men were fed six pints of beer each, within a one hour period.

It was then observed that 100% of the men gained weight, talked excessively without making sense, became overly emotional, couldn't drive, failed to think rationally, argued over nothing and refused to apologise when they were wrong.

IRISH FISHING JOKES

Patrick and Murphy were out fishing and the boat's motor quit.

Patrick says to Murphy, 'What are we going to do now?'

Murphy says, 'We'll just have to wait for help.'

After two days they are 90 km from the coast and come across a bottle. Patrick opens the bottle and out pops a genie who offers to grant them one wish.

Quick as a flash Patrick says, 'Turn the sea into Guinness!' and immediately the sea is black with Guinness.

Murphy says, 'You stupid fool! Now we'll have to piss in the boat!'

Bart was trapped in a bog and seemed a goner when Big Mick O'Reilly wandered by.

'Help!' Bart shouted, 'I'm sinking'!'

Don't worry,' assured Mick. 'Next to the Strong Muldoon, I'm the strongest man in Erin. I can out-muscle, out-spit, out-fish and out-box anyone and I'll pull ye right out o' there.'

Mick leaned out and grabbed Bart's hand and pulled and pulled to no avail.

After two more unsuccessful attempts, Mick said to Bart, 'Sure and I can't do it. The Strong Muldoon could do it alone, maybe, but I'll have to get some help.'

As Mick was leaving, Bart called 'Mick! Mick! Do you think it will help if I pull me feet out of the stirrups?'

Quinn was visiting his Irish cousin, Bannon. While there, he decided to do a bit of fishing.

As he sat there one afternoon, his cousin walked by. 'What are ye doing?' asked Bannon.

'Fishing,' said Quinn.

'Caught anything?'

'Ach, nae a bite.'

'What are ye using for bait?'

'Worms.'

'Let me see it,' said O'Bannon.

Quinn lifted the line from the water and handed it to his cousin.

O'Bannon took out his flask of whisky and dipped the worm in it.

He handed it back to Quinn, who cast his line once more.

As soon as the worm hit the water, his rod bent over double, the line screaming out.

'Have you got a bite?' asked O'Bannon.

'No!' shouted Quinn, fighting with the rod, 'The worm's got a salmon by the throat!'

Paddy Flaherty loved to fish and then go to the pub. He came home drunk every evening towards ten.

The missus was never too happy about it.

So one night she hides in the cemetery and figures to scare him. As poor Pat wanders by, up from behind a tombstone she jumps in a red devil costume screaming, 'Paddy Sean Flaherty, sure and you don't give up your drinking and it's to hell I'll take ye.'

Pat, undaunted, staggered back and demanded, 'Who the hell are you?'

To that the missus replied, 'I'm the devil, you damned old fool.'

To which Flaherty remarked, 'Damned glad to meet you sir, I'm married to your sister.'

JUST FOR FUN

Two old mates are on a fishing trip.

One morning, one of them keels over and dies, but the other decides to keep fishing, as the fish are still biting.

After he finishes, he cleans his catch and puts his mate in the back of his 4WD.

After driving for 36 hours, he thinks he better tell the cops about his mate, so he pulls into Carnarvon and tells the sergeant.

The sergeant listens to his story and says, 'Gee, he must be on the nose by now!'

The old bloke shakes his head and says, 'Nah I gilled and gutted him. He should be right for another 24 hours.'

A man was fishing for trout beside a golf links.

He hooked a beauty and was so excited that he tossed the fish over his head.

It came off the hook and flew onto the golf course.

While he was looking for it a golfer asked him what he was doing.

The fisherman replied: 'Looking for trout. They often leave the water and wriggle around the grass looking for grasshoppers.'

As he spoke, he picked up his missing trout.

For the rest of the day there were golfers up and down the river bank looking for trout.

Very early one morning, there was a soft knock on the door and a whisper, 'Wanna go fishing Ned ?'

'Little early, isn't it Billy Joe?'

'What, for fishing?'

'*No*, for stupid questions.'

One afternoon, two worms were crawling through the grass. The male worm said to female worm, 'How about if you and I go back to your place?'

The female worm said, 'Okay.' So, the two worms went back to her place. Then, the male worm noticed that the female worm is wearing a wedding ring.

The male worm said, 'I'm sorry honey, but I don't do this sort of thing with married worms.'

The female worm replied, 'Don't worry. My husband is not coming home.'

The male worm asked, 'How do you know that for sure?'

The female worm answered, 'Well, he got up early this morning and went fishing.'

LET ME OFF!

YOU KNOW THAT YOU'VE PICKED THE WRONG CHARTER FISHING BOAT, WHEN THE FISHERMAN:

1. Has the engine manual sitting open on the console next to the controls.
2. Screams 'Yeehaa!' as he turns the boat away from the dock and pushes the throttle forward.
3. Thinks it's an asset that he can drive so fast that he gets the boat completely out of the water.
4. Takes two hours and 25 minutes to reach your fishing destination on a five hour charter.
5. Can't stop laughing when he realises that his brother the cop gave you a speeding ticket on your way to his boat and says nothing about getting the ticket cancelled.
6. Casually tells you that on days he can't get a charter, he's a delivery driver for Pizza Hut.
7. Goes on for hours about how boats are safer than cars, but only because there are less boats to hit. He runs aground three times during this oration.
8. Goes on for hours about his alien abduction experiences, with much detail given to the tests they supposedly performed on him.
9. Other fishing guides hold up protective religious icons as he passes by.
10. At the end of the day's fruitless fishing, he begs you to allow him to use your name as a reference.

COOL THINGS FOR A FISHERMAN TO SAY:

- My son isn't an honour student, he plays hockey.
- Post Cool.
- Question appearances.
- Question authority.
- Question reality.
- Seen on the back of a biker's vest: if you can read this, my wife fell off.
- So many pedestrians, so little time.
- Subvert the dominant paradigm.
- This bumper sticker exploits illiterates.
- This is it, I don't have another car.
- 'This is Not an Abandoned Vehicle'—sticker on an old, rusted-out car with two plastic bags taped over where the rear windows used to be, parked in a shopping centre.
- Today's mood: irritable
- Warning! I brake for hallucinations.
- Warning: dates in calendar are closer than they appear.
- Welcome. Now. Go. Home.
- When everything's coming your way, you're in the wrong lane and going the wrong way.
- Your kid may be an honour student but you're still an idiot!

SCOTTISH FISHING AND HUNTING

Sandy MacLeod was charged with shooting a number of pigeons, the property of a Highland farmer.

The counsel for the defence tried to dissuade the old farmer.

'Now,' he remarked, 'are you prepared to swear that this man shot your pigeons?'

'I didn't say he shot them,' was the reply. 'I said that I suspected him of doing it.'

'Ah Now we're coming to it. What made you suspect it was Sandy?'

'Well, first, I caught him on my land with a gun. Secondly, I heard the gun go off and saw some pigeons fall. Thirdly, I found four of my pigeons in his sporran and I don't think the birds flew in there and then committed suicide.'

Sandy was on his way home from fishing late one night when a neighbour beckoned him for help.

'Here,' he said, 'give me a hand to get this pig out of the truck.'

When they had got the pig out of his truck, the neighbour said, 'Hold the pig still while I open the front door.'

Sandy quickly did as he was told and the neighbour said, 'Now help me push the pig upstairs.'

Sandy did that.

'Now,' he said, 'help me put the pig in the bathtub.'

After a great deal of effort they managed to put the pig in the bath.

'Look,' said Sandy, 'what is going on? Why do you need to put a huge pig in the bathtub?'

'I suppose you're entitled to an explanation,' said the neighbour. 'You see the problem is with my wife—she's one of those women who always knows everything. No matter what I tell her, she says to me, "I know, I know".'

'But how is a pig in the bath going to help?' asked Sandy.

'Well, tomorrow morning,' said the neighbour, 'she's going to rush into the bedroom and scream at me, 'There's a huge pig in the bath' and I'm going to lay back in bed and say to her, '"I know, I know".'

This fisherman went to a Scottish doctor and said, 'Doctor, I've got a very poor memory. What do you advise?'

'Well,' said the doc, 'for a start you can pay me in advance.'

Sandy was driving his young son home after a long day out fishing . . .

As they passed a hot dog stand, he sighed, 'My, those hot dogs smell really nice.'

'Hold on a moment,' said Sandy with great gallantry. 'I'll drive a little closer so you can get a better smell.'

Two shipwrecked Scottish fishermen had been hanging on for hours to an upturned boat.

Jock, realising that he might not be able to hold out much longer, began to recount his past misdeeds and to vow that if he escaped he would in future lead an entirely new life.

Suddenly, there was a cry from his comrade in distress: 'Wait, Jock! Don't commit yourself—I think I see land!'

An Englishman was being tried for being drunk and disorderly.

The judge asked him where he had bought the whisky.

'But I didn't buy it, Your Honour,' said the Englishman. 'A Scotsman gave it to me.'

'Fourteen days for perjury,' said the judge.

A Highlander stopped before a grave in the village cemetery, containing a carved tombstone declaring: 'Here lies a fisherman and an honest man . . .'

'And, who would ever think,' the Highlander murmured, 'there would be room enough for two men in that one wee grave.'

The fisherman was boring everyone in the highland pub to death.

He kept talking about a sea voyage to Africa, which interested no one.

'The waves were fifty feet high,' he said, 'I was at sea 30 years and never saw them that high.'

'Ah, well,' said one old highlander, 'waves are much higher now than they used to be.'

Sandy and Jock, enjoying an afternoon of fishing, were seated by the banks of the River Tay.

'Say,' said Jock, 'We're best friends; if you suddenly found a million dollars would you lend me ten thousand?'

'That depends,' said Sandy. 'What collateral have you got?'

A Scottish fisherman is the only man in the world who will step over the bodies of a dozen naked women to get to a glass of whisky.

'I have a very unusual Scottish watch to offer you. It never needs a battery or any winding. It has no hands and no face of any kind.'

'But how can you tell time?'

'That's easy. Ask anybody.'

To catch the fish, it's not how you throw the bait, but how you wiggle your worm.

Fishing rule #1: The least experienced fisherman always catches the biggest fish.

Fishing rule #2: The worse your line is tangled, the better is the fishing around you.

Fishing rule #3: Fishing will do a lot for a man, but it won't make him truthful.

A Highland proprietor of a sportsmen's lodge had advertised it 'to let', before going abroad. He instructed his gamekeeper to give it a favourable reputation when inquiries were received from any prospective tenants.

The first inquirer was an English sportsman and he naturally asked how the place was stocked.

'Are there any deer?'

'Oh yes,' replied the keeper, 'Thousands of them.'

A little suspicious, the visitor again inquired, 'And I suppose there are plenty of grouse?'

'Yes, sir,' came the ready assurance, 'Thousands of them as well.'

'And pheasants?'

'Yes indeed—thousands of pheasants.'

Thinking it time to put a stop to these wild estimates, the English visitor asked if there were any gorillas.

'Well,' came the cautious reply, 'They are not just so plentiful. They do come rarely, you know, just like yourself.'

SLOW DAY?

A FISHERMAN'S PHILOSOPHY

A sure way to get a bite on a slow day is:

- Talk about changing spots.
- Prepare another rod while one is out.
- Lay your rod down unsecured.
- Go for a sandwich.
- Start to pull the boat anchor.
- Use the worst fly you own.
- Crack open your first beer.
- Crack open your last beer.
- Take notice of the chick on a passing boat, bank or beach.
- Watch others fishing.
- Start reeling in your lines at going home time.
- Give your fishing rod to a female companion or child to hold.
- When your landing net is out of reach.
- When you have cast your line over an obstruction.
- When your line has drifted into impossible weeds.
- When you turn to look at the sunrise or sunset.
- Decide that you need to take a leak.

SMARTER THAN YOU THINK

Did you hear about the fisherman with the gambling problem?

He denied he had a problem and made a bet that he could give it up.

The old fisherman never shed a tear when his wife of forty years died suddenly.

He was in the pub shortly after having a quiet ale when his mate asked him how he was coping.

'Oh, I'm over it all now,' he said, 'It isn't as if she was a blood relation.'

At a pub in the country, one of the favourite pastimes of the patrons was to offer the village simpleton the choice between a shiny new 50 cent piece and a shaggy old ten dollar note.

The young lad would deliberate and think about it but, in the end, he always chose the shiny new coin.

As the story of the lad and his inevitable choices became known around the district, more people came to the pub to have a laugh at the boy's expense.

Bus tours would stop by the pub and the tourists would get out and offer the boy the choice of the shiny coin or the battered note.

He always chose the coin.

His uncle, who was fond of the boy, had enough of their smug laughter and took the lad aside.

'Jimmy, I just don't understand. You are not as silly as you make out and I'm sure you know the difference in value between a 50 cent piece and a $10 note. Why do you keep choosing the 50 cents?'

'Well, uncle, it's like this. How long do you think this choosing business would go on once I choose the $10 note? Nobody would offer me the bloody coin again . . .'

An Englishman was holding forth at the fishing club bar. 'I was born an Englishman. All my life I have been an Englishman and when I die I shall die an Englishman.'

An Irish voice from the other end of the bar piped in with, 'Have you no ambition, then?'

A fisherman was telling the whole bar about his lineage. 'I can trace my line right back to Noah's ark,' he boasted.

Not to be outdone, another came in with, 'At the time of the great floods, my family had their own boat.'

During outbreaks of fever, it is wise to filter and boil your drinking water.

Just to be on the safe side, however, drink whisky.

The parson was in full flight.

'When judgement day comes,' he thundered, 'there will be weeping and gnashing of teeth.'

'I don't have teeth,' called a drunk who had slunk into the back seat for a little shelter.

'Teeth will be provided,' returned the minister.

The wife returned from shopping for provisions for the week: six bottles of whisky and a loaf of bread.

Her husband, well known for taking a tipple in the fishing boat, shouted at her angrily, 'What in the name of the lord did you bring all that bread for, woman?'

The old fisherman was on the pier and next to him sat a clergy man.

He pulled out a bottle of whisky in a brown paper bag and took a drink from it.

Unable to contain himself, the reverend said, 'I'm 65 years old and never a drop of that stuff has passed my lips.'

'And it won't today either,' replied the fisherman, taking another swig.

The fisherman fell into the huge tank containing half a dozen man-eating sharks.

He survived the ordeal because he was wearing a t-shirt which read 'England for the World Cup'.

Not even the sharks would swallow that!

The drunk arrived at the parson's home late at night in a state of considerable intoxication.

'Reverend,' he said, 'I'm worried about the doctrine of predetermination.'

'Look,' said the minister, 'why don't you come back when you are sober?'

'Because, when I'm sober, I don't give a shit about predetermination.'

Two young football fans were travelling to Rome to support their team and were making arrangements as to where to meet.

'Let's meet at the Vatican,' said the first.

'In the bar or the lounge?' asked the second.

The weekly fishing bar raffle was won by a patron who had never won anything in his life before.

The prize was a toilet brush.

Midweek and he was back in the bar when the barman asked, 'And how do you like your new toilet brush?'

'Well I don't like it much at all. I think I'll go back to using toilet paper.'

Q: Have you heard about the fisherman who was suffering from alcoholic constipation?

A: He couldn't pass a pub.

The drunk, feeling religious fervour and full of the drink, hurled a bottle of bleach through the side door of the local church.

He was fined for bleach of the priest.

Three fishing mates had enjoyed drinking in the same place at the same pub for many years.

One day one of them came with the bad news that he didn't have much time left and that when he died, he would like them all to buy him a whisky and pour it on his grave.

There was silence as his mates contemplated the idea.

Then one spoke.

'Would it not be better if we gave it a good swill around our kidney first?'

The wife woke to the sound of her husband, having returned from an evening fishing. He was searching clumsily around the room, knocking furniture about.

'What are you looking for?' she asked.

'Nothing,' came the reply.

'Then you'll find it in the whisky bottle.'

The fisherman died and was met by St Peter at the pearly gates.

'You have told too many lies to get in here,' said St Peter.

'Have a heart,' came the reply, 'You were a fisherman once yourself.'

The fisherman down on his luck phoned up a friend and asked for a loan of ten dollars.

'Sorry! You'll have to speak up, I can't hear what you're saying,' said the friend.

'Can you lend me ten dollars?'

'I'm terribly sorry but the line is noisy, I can't hear a word you're saying.'

At this stage the operator chipped in with, 'There's nothing wrong with the line. I can hear everything quite distinctly.'

'In that case, you can lend him the ten quid.'

Two mates were doing a quiz while sitting out in the bay waiting for a bite.

The first question was, 'If you have 33 dollars in one pocket and 61 dollars in the other, what would you have?'

'Somebody else's trousers,' was the reply.

The second question was, 'If the National Gallery was on fire and you had the opportunity to save one painting, which one would you save?'

'The one closest to the door.'

The third question was, 'If you had ten dollars and I asked you for six. How much would you have?'

'Ten.'

Graffiti on the jetty:
DRINK IS YOUR ENEMY

Written next to it:
LOVE YOUR ENEMY

One fisherman to another:
'My wife is a sex object. Every time I want sex, she objects.'

An Englishman, an Irishman and a Scotsman went to the pub together.

The Englishman spent ten pounds, the Irishman spent seven pounds and the Scot had an excellent afternoon out.

The old fisherman carried his inebriated mate into an AA Meeting.

'He's drunk,' came a stern voice. You can't bring him in here. This is an AA Meeting.'

'Don't worry. He's far too drunk to notice.'

THE FISH WAS SO BIG THAT . . .

First fisherman:	'I went fishing and caught a 120 kg bluefish.'
Second fisherman:	'I was fishing from a boat when my line snagged an old pirate ship. In working my line free, I brought up an old ship's lantern and the candle was still lit!'
First fisherman:	'I'll take 100 kilos off my bluefish if you blow out that candle!'

First fisherman:	'Yeah, I saw a picture of that fish and he was all of 10 cm long.'
Second fisherman:	'Yeah, but after battling for three hours, a fish can lose a lot of weight.'

He caught a fish that was so big he took a picture of it and the negative weighed five kilos.

The water in that river is so polluted that if you catch a trout, he thanks you.

I catch deformed fish.
The ones I get always have their heads too close to their tails.

First fisherman: Just how big was that monster bream that got away from you, Denny?
Second fisherman: Well, I had 50 m of new line on my reel. I dropped the line over the side and the bream grabbed the bait and took off upstream. The last of the line ran off the reel just as the bream's tail passed the boat.

A fisherman had a visitor he hadn't seen for some time. The man noticed that there was now a glass case over the mantelpiece containing a large fish.

He asked about it.

'I got it on my last fishing trip. I was on my own in this little rowboat and I fought him for several hours before I got him aboard. Then he thrashed around so much I thought the boat would tip over. I can't swim a stroke and we'd drifted out so far I had to kill him with my bare hands. It was either me or the fish.'

'Well, I must say the fish makes a better decoration.'

A farmer was telling a couple of visitors: 'I keep telling my kids not to go fishing in the river. The cod there are so big the little blighters can't hold them. On Tuesday I lost one about three foot six long and yesterday I lost one more than four feet long.'

'My word. It's really bad luck losing fish that size.'

'Fish nothing! It's kids I'm losing.'

The day was fine, the sun was warm, but the fish were not biting at all. An angler who had spent the best part of the afternoon getting no result was asked by a local boy: 'How many fish have you caught?'

'None. And I've been here three hours.'

'Well, that's not so bad. One fellow fished here for three weeks and didn't catch any more than you've caught in three hours.'

THE SECRET OF LIFE

An American investment banker was at the pier of a small coastal Mexican village when a small boat with just one fisherman docked.

Inside the small boat were several large yellow fin tuna.

The American complimented the Mexican on the quality of his fish and asked how long it took to catch them.

The Mexican replied, 'Only a little while.'

The American then asked, 'Why didn't you stay out longer and catch more fish?'

The Mexican said, 'With this I have more than enough to support my family's needs.'

The American then asked, 'But what do you do with the rest of your time?'

The Mexican fisherman said, 'I sleep late, fish a little, play with my children, take siesta with my wife, Maria and stroll into the village each evening where I sip wine and play guitar with my amigos. I have a full and busy life.'

The American scoffed, 'I am a Harvard MBA and could help you. You should spend more time fishing; and with the proceeds, buy a bigger boat. With the proceeds from the bigger boat you could buy several boats. Eventually you would have a fleet of fishing boats. Instead of selling your catch to a middleman you would sell directly to the processor; eventually opening your own cannery. You would control the product, processing and distribution. You would need to leave this small coastal fishing village and move to Mexico City, then Los Angeles and eventually New York where you will run your ever-expanding enterprise.'

The Mexican fisherman asked, 'But, how long will this all take?'

To which the American replied, '15 to 20 years.'

'But what then?' asked the Mexican.

The American laughed and said that's the best part.

'When the time is right you would announce an IPO and sell your company stock to the public and become very rich. You would make millions.'

'Millions? Then what?'

The American said, 'Then you would retire. Move to a small coastal fishing village where you would sleep late, fish a little, play with your kids, take siesta with your wife, stroll to the village in the evenings where you could sip wine and play your guitar with your amigos.'

A man was sick and tired of going to work every day while his wife stayed at home and complained whenever he wanted to go fishing.

He wanted her to see what he went through, so he prayed.

'I want her to know what I go through, so please create a trade in our bodies.'

God in his infinite wisdom granted the man's wish.

The next morning, sure enough, the man awoke as a woman.

He arose, cooked breakfast for his mate, awakened the kids, set out their school clothes, fed them breakfast, packed their lunches, drove them to school, came home and picked up the dry cleaning, took it to the cleaners and stopped at the bank to draw out money to pay the power and the telephone bills, drove to both companies and paid the bills, went grocery shopping, came home and put the groceries away.

Then it was already 1 pm. He hurried to make the beds, do the laundry, vacuum, dust, sweep and mop the kitchen floor.

He ran to school to pick up the kids and got into an argument with them on the way home.

Set out cookies and milk and got the kids organised to do their homework, then set up the ironing board and watched TV while he did the ironing.

At 4.30 pm he began peeling the potatoes and washing the greens for salad, breaded the pork chops and snapped the fresh beans for supper.

After supper he cleaned the kitchen, ran the dishwasher, folded the laundry, bathed the kids and put them to bed.

At 9 pm he was exhausted and though his chores weren't finished yet, he went to bed where he was expected to make love, which he managed to get through without complaint.

The next morning he awoke and immediately knelt by the bed and said, 'Lord I don't know what I was thinking, I was so wrong to envy my wife, being able to stay at home all day. Please, oh please, let us trade back.'

The Lord in his infinite wisdom again, replied, 'My son. I feel you have learned your lesson and I will be happy to change things back to the way they were. But you'll have to wait nine months though, because you got pregnant last night.'

TRUISMS ABOUT FISHING

Work is for those who don't fish.

Fish now. You are dead a long time.

Some fishermen catch their best fish by the tale.

Noah never fished from his Ark because he only had two worms.

Only dead fish swim with the current.

No man, having caught a very large fish, returns home via an alley.

Not all fishermen are liars, but a lot of liars are fishermen.

Not all men are fools, some are fishermen.

Fishermen are born honest, but they grow out of it.

The length of the fish grows the more time that elapses between catching and telling.

I don't exaggerate, my memory just magnifies things.

A man who can't wait ten minutes for a woman, can often wait all day for a fish.

The truth is told when one fisherman calls the other a liar.

God counts the days spent fishing as days of worship.

If you caught fish every time you went out, they would call it 'catching'.

It is better to sit in your boat and to think about God, than to sit in Church and think about fishing.

God invented fishing to keep the truly gifted from ruling the world.

I used to have a handle on my life, then my rod broke.

Old fishermen never die, they just smell that way.

The trouble with fishing is that it is always better before you get there and after you leave.

Give a man a fish and feed him for a day. Teach a man to fish and he will sit in a boat and drink beer all day.

I spent most of my life fishing, the rest I wasted.

Fishing is a jerk on one end of the line waiting for a jerk on the other end!

The worst day of fishing beats the best day of work.

THINGS TO THINK ABOUT WHILE FISHING:

- Never take a sleeping pill and a laxative on the same night.
- Never lick a steak knife.
- Take out the fortune before you eat the fortune cookie.
- Is it okay to pick your nose . . . if no one sees you flip the bugger?
- Should you always offer to bait your date's hook . . . if this is your first fishing date?
- Is it okay for the dog to eat at the table . . . if he has good table manners?

PONDERINGS

THINGS TO THINK ABOUT WHEN YOU ARE WETTING A LINE:

- Can you cry under water?
- When I was young we used to go 'skinny dipping,' now I just 'chunky dunk'.
- How important does a person have to be before they are considered assassinated instead of just murdered?
- If money doesn't grow on trees then why do banks have branches?
- Why do you have to 'put your two cents in' . . . but it's only 'a penny for your thoughts?' Where's that extra penny going to?
- Once you're in heaven, do you get stuck wearing the clothes you were buried in for eternity?

- Why does a round pizza come in a square box?
- How is it that we put man on the moon before we figured out it would be a good idea to put wheels on luggage?
- Why is it that people say they 'slept like a baby' when babies wake up every two hours?
- If a deaf person has to go to court, is it still called a hearing?
- Why are you *in* a movie, but you are *on* TV?
- Why do people pay to go up tall buildings and then put money in binoculars to look at things on the ground?
- How come we choose from just two people for President and fifty for Miss America? Shouldn't they have to parade down the runway wearing a skimpy swim suit before we have to vote on them?
- If a 000 operator has a heart attack, whom does he or she call?
- Why is it when I signed up for an exercise class I was told to wear loose-fitting clothing? If I *had* any loose-fitting clothing, I wouldn't have signed up in the first place!
- Wouldn't it be nice if whenever we messed up our life we could simply press 'Ctrl, Alt, Delete', and start all over?
- Stress is when you wake up screaming and then you realise you haven't fallen asleep yet.
- The human heart creates enough pressure when it pumps out to the body to squirt blood 30 feet.
- A pig's orgasm lasts 30 minutes.
- A cockroach will live nine days without its head before it starves to death.
- Banging your head against a wall uses 150 calories an hour.
- The male praying mantis cannot copulate while its head

is attached to its body. The female initiates sex by ripping the male's head off.

- The flea can jump 350 times its body length. It's like a human jumping the length of a football field.
- The catfish has over 27,000 taste buds.
- Some lions mate over 50 times a day.
- Butterflies taste with their feet.
- The strongest muscle in the body is the tongue.
- Right-handed people live, on average, nine years longer than left-handed people.
- Elephants are the only animals that cannot jump.
- A cat's urine glows under a black light.
- An ostrich's eye is bigger than its brain.
- Starfish have no brains.
- Polar bears are left-handed.
- Humans and dolphins are the only species that have sex for pleasure.

RELAX!!!

JOKES TO TELL WHILE YOU'RE FISHING

The long term implications of current drugs, medical procedures and priorities over the past few years, more money has been spent on breast implants and Viagra than on Alzheimer's Disease research.

As a consequence, the medical research now estimates that by the year 2030 there will be 40 million people wandering around with huge breasts and erections, who can't remember what to do with them.

A local business was looking for office help. They put a sign in the window, stating the following: 'HELP WANTED. Must be able to type, must be good with a computer and must be bilingual. We are an Equal Opportunity Employer.'

A short time afterwards, a dog trotted up to the window, saw the sign and went inside.

He looked at the receptionist and wagged his tail, then walked over to the sign, looked at it and whined.

Getting the idea, the receptionist got the office manager.

The office manager looked at the dog and was surprised, to say the least.

However, the dog looked determined, so he led him into the office. Inside, the dog jumped up on the chair and stared at the manager.

The manager said, 'I can't hire you. The sign says you have to be able to type.'

The dog jumped down, went to the typewriter and proceeded to type out a perfect letter.

He took out the page and trotted over to the manager and gave it to him, then jumped back on the chair.

The manager was stunned, but then told the dog, 'The sign says you have to be good with a computer.'

The dog jumped down again and went to the computer.

The dog proceeded to enter and execute a perfect program, that worked flawlessly the first time.

By this time the manager was totally dumbfounded!

He looked at the dog and said, 'I realise that you are a very intelligent dog and have some interesting abilities. However, I still can't give you the job.'

The dog jumped down and went to a copy of the sign and put his paw on the sentences that told about being an Equal Opportunity Employer.

The manager said, 'Yes, but the sign also says that you have to be bilingual'.

The dog looked at the manager calmly and said, 'Meow.'

One day in the future, George W. Bush has a heart attack and dies.

He immediately goes to hell, where the devil is waiting for him.

'I don't know what to do here,' says the devil. 'You are on my list, but I have no room for you. You definitely have to stay here, so I'll tell you what I'm going to do. I've got a couple folks here who weren't quite as bad as you. I'll let one of them go, but you have to take their place. I'll even let you decide who leaves.'

Bush thought that sounded pretty good, so the devil opened the first room. In it was Richard Nixon and a large pool of water. He kept diving in and surfacing empty handed. Over and over and over. Such was his fate in hell.

'No,' George said. 'I don't think so. I'm not a good swimmer and I don't think I could do that all day long.'

The devil led him to the next room.

In it was Newt Gingrich with a sledgehammer and a room full of rocks.

All he did was swing that hammer, time after time after time.

'No, I've got this problem with my shoulder. I would be in constant agony if all I could do was break rocks all day,' commented George.

The devil opened a third door.

In it, Bush saw Bill Clinton, lying on the floor with his arms staked over his head and his legs staked in a spread eagle pose.

Bent over him was Monica Lewinsky, doing what she does best.

Bush took this in in disbelief and finally said, 'Yeah, I can handle this. This is the place for me.'

The devil smiled and said, 'Okay, Monica, you're free to go.'

Bush and Powell were sitting in a bar. A guy walked in and asked the barman, 'Isn't that Bush and Powell?'

The barman said, 'Yep, that's them.'

So the guy walked over and said, 'Hello. What are you guys doing?'

Bush said, 'We're planning World War III.'

The guy asked, 'Really? What's going to happen?'

Bush said, 'Well, we're going to kill 10 million Afghans and one bicycle repairman.'

The guy exclaimed, 'Why are you gonna kill a bicycle repairman?!'

Bush turned to Powell and said, 'See, I told you no one would worry about the 10 million Afghans!'

Several women appeared in court, each accusing the others of causing the trouble they were having in the apartment building where they lived.

The women were arguing noisily even in the court.

The judge, banging his gavel to quiet them said, 'We are going to do this in an orderly manner. I can't listen to all of you at once. I'll hear the oldest first.'

The case was dismissed for lack of testimony . . .

By the time a Marine pulled into a little town, every hotel room was taken.

'You've got to have a room somewhere,' he pleaded. 'Or even just a bed, I don't care where.'

'Well, I do have a double room with one occupant, an Air Force guy,' admitted the manager, 'And he might be glad to split the cost.'

'But to tell you the truth, he snores so loudly that people in adjoining rooms have complained in the past. I'm not sure it'd be worth it to you.'

'No problem,' the tired Marine assured him. 'I'll take it.'

The next morning the Marine came down to breakfast bright-eyed and bushy-tailed.

'How'd you sleep?' asked the manager.

'Never better.'

The manager was impressed. 'No problem with the other guy snoring, then?'

'Nope, I shut him up in no time' said the Marine.

'How'd you manage that?' asked the manager.

'He was already in bed, snoring away, when I came in the room,' the Marine explained.

'I went over, gave him a kiss on the cheek, said, "Goodnight, beautiful," and he sat up all night watching me.'

SPRUNG!

YOU KNOW THAT YOU ARE A FISHERMAN IF:

- You have a power worm dangling from your rear view mirror because you think it makes a good air freshener.
- Your wedding party had to tie tin cans to the back of your bass boat.
- You call your boat 'sweetheart' and your wife 'skeeter'.
- Your local tackle shop has your credit card number on file.
- You keep a flipping stick by your favourite chair to change the TV channels with.
- You name your black Labrador 'Mercury' and your cat 'Evinrude'.
- The local bait shop has a private line just for you.
- You have your name painted on a parking space at the launch ramp.
- You have a photo of your 10 lb bass on your desk at work instead of your family.
- You consider cold sausages and crackers a complete meal.
- You think 'megabytes' means a great day fishing.
- You send your kid off to the first day of school with his shoes tied in a palomar knot.
- You think there are four seasons—Pre-spawn, Spawn, Post Spawn and Hunting.
- Your $30,000 bass boat's trailer needs new tyres so you just 'borrow' the ones off your caravan.

- You trade your wife's van for a smaller vehicle so your boat will fit in the garage.
- Your kids know it is Saturday—because the boat's gone.

21ST CENTURY FISHERMAN

YOU KNOW YOU'RE A FISHERMAN LIVING IN 2004 WHEN . . .

- You accidentally enter your password on the microwave.
- You haven't played solitaire with real cards in years.
- You have a list of 15 phone numbers to reach your family of three.
- You e-mail the person who works at the desk next to you.
- Your reason for not staying in touch with friends is that they don't have e-mail addresses.
- When you go home after a long day at work you still answer the phone in a business manner.
- When you make phone calls from home, you accidentally dial '9' to get an outside line.
- You've sat at the same desk for four years and worked for three different companies.
- You learn about your redundancy on the 11 o'clock news.
- Your boss doesn't have the ability to do your job.
- Contractors outnumber permanent staff and are more likely to get long-service awards.
- You read this entire list and kept nodding and smiling.
- As you read this list, you think about forwarding it to your friends.
- You got this e-mail from a friend that never talks to you anymore, except to send you jokes from the net.

OOPS, SORRY!

THINGS THAT YOU SHOULD NEVER SAY IN A TACKLE SHOP:

- All right, who's going to be a sport and show me their favourite fishing hole?
- Anyone know who owns the red pick-up out front that I just hit?
- [Pointing to the merchandise.] Look at all this antique tackle.
- Let me tell you about a fish I once caught . . .
- What! No high-tech lures? How can you people catch anything?
- One of you has got to be named Bubba . . . let me guess.
- You do take travellers' cheques, don't you?
- Your rods look as if they were wrapped at the Lighthouse Project for the Blind.
- [Pointing to the photo on the wall.] Are those fish you caught or is that a family portrait?
- I only use imported hooks.
- I need a new rod. Do you have anything in blue to match my reel?
- [To the woman assistant.] Want to see my lure?
- You call this live bait? Why, where I'm from, we . . .

YOUNG FISHERMEN

David burst into the house, crying.
His mother comforted him and asked him what the problem was.

'Daddy and I were fishing,' he sobbed, 'And he hooked a giant fish. Really big. Then, while he was reeling it in, the line busted and the fish got away.'

'Now come on, David,' his mother said, 'A big boy like you shouldn't be crying about an accident like that. You should have just laughed it off.'

'But that's just what I did, mummy . . .'

It was a cold winter day.

An old man walked out onto a frozen lake, cut a hole in the ice, dropped in his fishing line and waited patiently for a bite.

He was there for almost an hour, without even a nibble, when a young boy walked out onto the ice, cut a hole in the ice next to him.

The young boy dropped his fishing line and minutes later he hooked a Largemouth Bass.

The old man couldn't believe his eyes but put it down to plain luck.

Shortly thereafter, the young boy pulled in another large catch.

The young boy kept catching fish after fish. Finally, the old man couldn't take it any longer.

'Son,' he said,'I've been here for over an hour without even a nibble. You've been here only a few minutes and have caught a half dozen fish! How do you do it?'

The boy responded,'Roo raf roo reep ra rums rarrm.'

'What was that?' the old man asked.

Again the boy responded,'Roo raf roo reep ra rums rarrm.'

'Look,' said the old man,'I can't understand a word you're saying.'

The boy spat the bait into his hand and said . . .'You have to keep the worms warm!'

An old man rocking on his porch sees a young kid and his fishing rod walking down the dirt road.

'Where you going with that fishing rod?' he calls.

'Gonna git me some fish with this here fishing pole!' answers the kid.

Sure enough, as the sun is setting the old man sees the kid going home with a bucket of fish.

Next day, the old man rocking on his porch sees the kid walking down the road with some duct tape.

'Where you going with that?' he calls.'Gonna git me some ducks with this here duct tape!' answers the kid.

'You can't git no ducks with tape!' hollers the old man.

But sure enough, as the sun is setting the old man sees the kid going home with the tape strung out behind him and ducks stuck all over it!

Next day, the old man rocking on his porch sees the kid

walking down the dirt road with some chicken wire.

'Where you going with that?' he calls. 'Gonna get me some chickens with this chicken wire!' answers the kid.

'You can't get no chickens with chicken wire!' hollers the old man.

But sure enough, as the sun is setting, the old man sees the kid going home with the wire strung out behind him and chickens stuck all through it!

Next day, the old man rocking on his porch sees the kid walking down the dirt road with some pussy willows.

'Now hold on just a minute,' calls the old man, 'Wait while I get my hat . . .!'